Toronto, February

Brian

The only good thing that anyone has told me is that I hope this book is entertaining, and, as you it entertains you as well, as you are recovering.

It took me 2500 hours at the word processor and will earn me a total of 10,000 dollars, so I worked below "minimum" for a year! It's expected to sell about 7000 copies, that's all. Business books, even in the US where this is published, sell only in a small amounts, except for the one in a million best-seller.

Anyway solving the puzzles in the book will keep you busy.

Warm regards,

Denn

# THE
# PARADOX
# PROCESS

"No matter how clearly aware we think we are of the necessity to explore unorthodox solutions to intractable problems, many (if not most) of us remain prisoners of convention and of our background. And opportunities pass us by. Derm Barrett jolts us out of our preconceptions: It is impossible to read *The Paradox Process* without taking a new look at old quandaries and widening our focus for the next ones."

—Anthony Griffin, Guardian Capital Group

"I found *The Paradox Process* a fascinating book. Readers may well find themselves in a Janus-like position: They will buy the book for its practical management solutions but will soon find themselves devouring the book for sheer pleasure and mental enjoyment. This book entertains while it stretches the mind."

—George Miller, The Mining Association of Canada

"The concepts mentioned in this book are used here at Honeywell as we try to change the 'paradigm' of how we think. *The Paradox Process* contains many helpful tools and should be kept in a desk drawer for when you need to refocus your efforts."

—Ron Holmes, Manufacturing Engineering
Manager, Honeywell

"What appeals to me most about *The Paradox Process* is Dr. Barrett's use of examples that are practical, day-to-day applications of paradox—at work and at leisure—along with his brief exercises that provoke readers into exploring their own concepts of paradox. His book is, perhaps paradoxically, entertaining and educational."

—John Morrissey, Ph.D., Vice President,
Human Resources, AG Simpson

# THE
# PARADOX
# PROCESS

Creative Business Solutions . . .
Where You Least Expect to Find Them

## Derm Barrett

AMACOM
**American Management Association**
New York . Atlanta . Boston . Chicago . Kansas City . San Francisco . Washington, D.C.
Brussels . Mexico City . Tokyo . Toronto

**Library of Congress Cataloging-in-Publication Data**

Barrett, Derm.
    The paradox process : creative business solutions, where you least
expect to find them / Derm Barrett.
      p.  cm.
    Includes bibliographical references and index.
    ISBN 0-8144-0356-5
    1. Creative ability in business.   I. Title.   II. Title: Creative
business solutions, where you least expect to find them
    HD53.B37   1997
    650.1—dc21                             97-35051
                                                      CIP

All the ambigrams are © John Langdon except Edwards
Enterprises logo and Suburban Transit Network logo, which are
trademarks of those companies. Used by permission.

Printing number

10   9   8   7   6   5   4   3   2   1

To the memory
of
**Professor W. Rupert Maclaurin,**
Scholar and Teacher
of Economics and Innovation
at MIT, 1936–1959

# CONTENTS

# PREFACE AND PURPOSE

*The Paradox Process* is the culmination of my fifty-year quest for an understanding of change and innovation.

The quest began in 1948, when I was a twenty-four-year-old graduate student at MIT. I was taking part in Rupert Maclaurin's seminar entitled The Economics of Invention and Innovation. Never before or since has a teacher had such a profound and enduring effect on me.

Professor Maclaurin was a pioneer investigator of the part played by technology and innovation in economic growth and change. His seminar showed us how an economy grows as entrepreneurs and innovators seize hold of new inventions and ideas and use them to create new businesses. More than that, it showed us that the world we inhabit is largely man-made, in which we are surrounded by nothing but the products of human creativity and imagination, ranging from buildings, houses, and asphalted avenues to the planes in the sky and the subways running underground, the furnishings and equipment in our rooms and offices, the clothing on our bodies and the lenses on our eyes. Creativity is the music and sound we hear, the colors and designs we see, and the information and knowledge in print, images, and sound that help steer us through it all. As Professor Maclaurin pointed out, the human species was first, foremost, and last a creative species, a species that not only created for itself the immediate world it lived in but had not yet stopped doing so.

Among other things, we studied the human actors in the drama of economic evolution and the roles that they played. They fell into three categories: inventors, who discovered, created, and invented new products or services; innovators, who put the new products or services into successful application, and entrepreneurs, who marshaled the money and organized the commercial enterprises that made innovation an economic success. Often the categories and the roles were blurred. Edison and Marconi not only invented and innovated but built hugely successful corporations, namely General Electric and the Marconi Wireless Telegraph Co., Ltd. Some inventors only invented, while others brought their inventions into application via the innovations process. Still others created the enterprises within which the inventors and innovators could do their work. Sometimes inventors invented better schemes of organization, production, and management, as did Henry Ford, Frederick Taylor, Frank Gilbreth, and Alfred Sloan. Other kinds of inventors and innovators came up with new services and conveniences, such as drive-in theaters, motels, and supermarkets.

All the roles played by the actors in the drama of change and innovation are creative roles. The actors have no script to follow. They create their own play and execute their own lines. What is clear is that an economy is creativity at work. Creativity is the propeller that drove the ship of progress. Yet many of our organizations today, business as well as nonbusiness, perform no such function and display zero creativity. They are bureaucracies stultifying progress, improvement, and the life force. They are enterprises in senility, managed by administrators whose passion is order and control. Everything has its opposite, and they are the opposite.

To show the processes of invention and innovation at work, Professor Maclaurin trotted us around to chat with brilliant local inventors, such as Edwin Land. Land left Harvard after his first year, on the grounds that it had been interfering with his education by not enabling him to learn fast enough. He formed his own corporation to do research and development in the field of optics. In 1933, Land invented polarization and polarized sunglasses, and in 1943, instant photography, the inspiration for which came from his five-year-old daughter. While they were vacationing in Mexico, she asked him, "Daddy, why can't I see the pictures right away?"

Professor Maclaurin brought us to the Raytheon Company. The company was developing a device it then called a radar oven. An engineer working near military radar equipment discovered that radar waves (microwaves) had melted a chocolate bar in his pocket. That melted bar was destined to give us the microwave oven.

The professor brought us to other places too, since we happened to be conveniently situated in one of the geographical hubs of American high-tech entrepreneurship. Nothing inspired the conviction that creativity is everything than these visits to these real-life inventors and innovative companies. The pattern was crystal clear: Creativity produces new innovations and new innovations produce economic growth and change.

By giving us this inside look and bringing us face-to-face with great innovators, Professor Maclaurin enabled us to see that industrial change and progress come out of the minds of human beings who dream and think and imagine, giving birth to new products or services—indeed, to whole new industries. I saw that while we can see what inventors, innovators, and entrepreneurs do because what they do is visible, we cannot see the thoughts, dreams, and ideas in their minds that enable them to do what they do. If we could learn more about the minds of these actors—and the mental processes of discovery, invention, and innovation—we ought to be able to help anyone who aspires to be more creative to actually become more creative.

In the many years since I left the early inspirational years of school behind me, and worked as a management teacher and consultant, or as a practicing manager, my main mission has been to help organizations and individuals reap the great advantages that come from being innovative. The desire to help people discover their own creative powers, to motivate them to make use of them, and to facilitate their efforts has been carried to Europe and South America as well as Canada and the United States. The success of clients and students has been my success, and their constant positive results have kept me going. Psychologists call it positive reinforcement and say that positive reinforcement is a powerful motivator. I think of a small company that saved itself from bankruptcy, of a large oil company that added $10 million a year to the net profits of one of its refineries, of a chemical company that reduced the cycle time on its new projects by half.

The fact is that the more I found out about how creative people could become with only a very small amount of help and advice, the more passionate I became about the business of creativity. Their successes confirmed that nothing is more natural to human beings than to be inventive and creative, and that once they realize this about themselves there is no stopping them. I cheerfully admit to having become a creativity zealot.

One of the purposes of this book is to describe and explain the creative process in a way that shows how natural it is, and to encourage readers to take advantage of the process in dealing with their personal and business challenges. Although the central focus of this book is on the *Paradox Process*—the method by which to achieve heightened creativity—it also contains my findings in the more general fields of change and innovation. These findings are derived from readings, observations, discussions, and personal experiences and experiments. The experience and experimentation have almost all been in the field of organization and management, both in the profit-driven sector and in not-for-profit parts of the economy, such as government departments, social agencies, professional associations, volunteer organizations, universities, and hospitals. I owe, therefore, a huge debt to all these sources and so many other people who have been as interested in change, innovation, and creativity as I have.

Only by drawing from such bountiful sources and experiences have I been able to pull together, construct, and synthesize the final product, namely the Paradox Process, together with the supporting methods and substantive content in this book. For these reasons, this book is not the singular product of any one mind. I would like to think that this is one of its merits.

Those who have contributed to this book include many philosophical thinkers who have thought stubbornly and persistently about opposites, paradoxes, and creativity, plus the psychologists, sociologists, economists, and historians who have written about change, innovation, organization, and management. A short listing of such thinkers would include Anaximander, Heraclitus, Zeno, Aristotle, Nietzsche, Fichte, Hegel, Bergson, Whitehead, and Koestler. The economists would include Rupert Mclaurin, Joseph Schumpeter, and Jacob Shmookler. Some of the psychologists whose insights on creativity have been the most helpful include Milton Erickson, Freud, Jung, Guilford, May, Maslow, Perls, and most recently and prominently, Harvard University's Albert Rothenberg. Albert Rothenberg's remarkable discovery—Janusian thinking—is explained in this book. His influence has been profoundly inspirational, with respect not only to Janusian thinking but also to the epistemological and onto-logical importance of opposites.

In addition, I have to thank many teachers and consultants who have spent their lives working in the field of creativity, change, and innovation. Others who have contributed to my learning process include numerous clients, among whom have been large companies like IBM, DuPont, Celanese, Alcan, Nortel, Bell, Hercules, General Foods, and Sara Lee, as well as small companies such as Dyeco in Kingston, Ontario, a company featured in this book. Such unwitting contributors include such geographically and industrially diverse groups as coffee growers in Colombia, construction firms in Argentina, investment companies in Brazil, management associations in Uruguay, railroaders in Spain, actuarial consultants in England, mining companies in Canada, and merchandising enterprises in the United States. There have also been public sector organizations such as hospitals, social agencies, police forces, armies and air forces, ecclesiastical organizations, universities, and municipal, provincial, and federal governments.

Professional associates and personal friends and relatives have been the most immediate and direct contributors. They have read drafts of the manuscript and given me suggestions, pointed out errors, and shared their thoughts. I want to express my heartfelt thanks to Teresa Anunza, Leslie Barrett, John Boyd, Burke Brown, Emile Carriere, Bill Christopher, Fran Donaldson, Carlos Ferrari, Mark Golding, Tony Griffin, Roy Jones, Dee and David Kramer, John and Claire Morrissey, Krista Muis, Helen Petrie, John Prior, John Sawatsky, and Leonard and Kathy Sayles.

John Prior, my neighbor and management consultant colleague, went over every chapter carefully with me, giving me his perspective on each, and helping me make important improvements, Dave Kramer, a nuclear physicist, assiduously instructed me in modern physics for many hours. Then, with all the patience of a saint, Dave helped me fumble, search for, and find startling opposites and paradoxes out there in the galactic wilderness of the stars and then down deep into the quirky never-never land of exotic and strange particles within the atom and its parts. The Morrisseys, who are both therapists and human resources experts, helped me search for and find examples of innovations in psychotherapeutic method that contain the concepts of opposites and paradox at their pivot.

Roy Jones, whose multidecade career has been exclusively devoted to helping business executives and professionals produce creative breakthroughs, helped me build the inventory of oxymorons and palindromes that are used in Chapter 10, the book's brain-trainer chapter. Krista Muis comforted me and cast her eagle eye over the entire project, looking for meaning, simplicity, clarity, validity, and consistency. My old classmate from MIT and close personal friend, Len Sayles, gave me constant encouragement as I struggled with a variety of conceptual and practical problems.

Bill Christopher, my colleague in The Management Innovations Group in Stamford, Connecticut, of which he is founder and president, has been with me on this project from its very beginning, week in and week out, right to its very end. Bill has provided me with unflagging help and a rich flow of inputs, examples of paradoxical innovations, and suggestions. I thank him also for the unstinting moral support he always made available whenever it wes needed.

My old friend and colleague Emile Carriere helped me enormously, particularly on Chapter 5, the key discussion of the paradox mind-set. For a month or more, he and I kept the fax lines burning between Toronto and his base in Burlington, Vermont, as we exchanged successive versions of it and other chapters. Emile insisted that the chapter take the reader carefully through the process in a concrete way that the reader could picture and adapt for his own use.

As always, my wife and colleague, Tina Barrett, has worked over every single paragraph and sentence with me. While the book was being created, over the last three years, Tina spent endless hours helping me to explore the world of opposites, contradictions, and paradox in every field under the sun, within the sun, and beyond the sun. In the process, she contributed a lot of valuable ideas and insights of which I have made good use. In addition, she helped me endlessly and patiently to engineer and reengineer the book's structure and flow. Without her, this book never would have been completed.

A special thanks is owed to John Langdon for being so generous in allowing me to use a large number of his ambigrams. These are visual-linguistic paradoxes, and so fit the aims of this book to a T. I have used them in Chapters 3, 6, and 10 as mind-training tools for readers to practice on. John is a philosopher of science, as well as an artist, teacher, and designer of typography and commercial logos. Our busy e-mail and fax correspondence enabled me to tie in with a creative mind deeply intrigued with the paradoxical features of reality as they have revealed themselves to him through his study of twentieth-century physics and Eastern philosophies.

Jacquie Flynn, development editor at AMACOM, helped me structure the chaotic material that constituted my first draft. There is no way of exaggerating what I owe her. My gratitude also to my copyeditor, Carole Berglie, who, among other things, so deftly moved sentences about and put paragraphs and ideas in their proper places.

Finally, I have to express my gratitude to those paradoxical thinkers in every field whose creativity has resulted in concrete examples of how paradoxical thinking is done and the benefits it produces.

# THE
# PARADOX
# PROCESS

# Chapter 1

# AN INTRODUCTION TO THE PARADOX PROCESS

"A great truth is one whose opposite is also a great truth."
—Thomas Mann

There has never been a time in history when our need for creative thinking has been greater than it is now. We live in a period characterized by profound and multitudinous problems, all requiring imaginative solutions. It can equally be said that there has never been a time when opportunities for creative innovation have been as plentiful as they are today. Ours is an age of almost unlimited creative possibilities. And imaginative thought and bold action are the twin keys for solving those problems and capitalizing on those opportunities. This book offers a powerful and comprehensive methodology for unlocking both. I call it the *Paradox Process*. It is a recipe for life in an era of hyperchange.

No matter how creative and innovative you have been, there are resources here that you can draw upon. The Paradox Process is a construction of several parts, some relatively new, some fairly old, and some ancient. It consolidates different creativity strategies and methods into a single pattern, in a manner that you can adapt for your own purposes. It opens you to new solutions by helping you identify opposite and contrary elements.

In the Paradox Process you have three options: You can encourage yourself to do or think the opposite of what is conventional; you can think and do two opposite things simultaneously, juxtaposing them in a creative new arrangement; or you can combine those opposites to form a new synthesis. Often, the best bet is to try all three strategies, in the expectation that one will give you your answer. By using the Paradox Process, you will find outlets for your creative energies. You will put yourself in the proper mind-set for making breakthroughs, coming up with inventive ideas, and producing creative innovations. You will significantly increase the quality and quantity of your efforts.

The Paradox Process is even more effective when applied to a team effort. You can set up cross-functional creativity teams of five to nine people at all levels, train them in the Paradox Process, and let them search for solutions to your organization's problems. Indeed, you will be surprised by what these teams can do. And when everyone in your organization is engaged in creative effort, the results are astonishing. The results will range from more creative corporate strategies to better operating mailrooms, from more powerful marketing strategies to more effective computer systems, and from a more energized workforce to a sharper board of directors. You'll see breakthrough achievements in quality, productivity, and customer service, in improved revenues, lower costs, and greater profits. When already able people add creativity to their repertoire of strategies, they demonstrate what they truly are capable of.

## *Release Your Innate Creativity*

Until now, society has been able to get by by asking a few people with special talents to create, invent, and innovate. The majority of people simply consumed or produced what was invented by someone else. But this system is no longer viable. Everyone has to get into the act.

Contrary to common belief, creativity does not just happen, it is made to happen. Moreover, anyone can learn to be more creative. Most people are surprised to find out that they can be creative. And they are especially impressed with how big the rewards of creativity can be. The collective and individual ingenuity of humankind, combined with drive and hard work, has already made incredible things possible. And having gone so far already, we are able to go further and make the world the way we really want it. That is not rhetoric, it is reality.

Don't associate the ability to create new solutions only with persons of great genius. Creative and inventive abilities are present in all people, to varying degrees. Research has shown that anyone who wants to be more creative can be. In fact, any business that wants to help people become more creative can cause impressive outpourings of valuable and practical creativity to take place.

All normal human beings, by sheer virtue of being human, have the inborn skill to be creative and inventive. Our ability to discover, create, and invent has been built into our brain through millions of years of evolution. Up until the age of five or six, most children show an urge to explore and experiment. But after this age, that urge often abates dramatically. Society, family, and our cultural institutions restrain most people to the point where the urge to innovate disappears from view. That creative spirit remains latent, however, and can be made to reappear.

## HOW THIS BOOK WILL HELP YOU

In small and large businesses where policies of empowerment and innovation are in place, *The Paradox Process* will help managers and employees become more enterprising and innovative. After everyone in the company has acquired its vocabulary and tools, the paradox mind-set will permeate the atmosphere of every department and unit. Within this corporate culture, creative productivity and breakthroughs both large and small will exceed anything anyone would have expected. But this book is equally designed for the increasing number of people who work as self-employed consultants and independent contractors. It is also intended for people whose work is to teach others the skills of entrepreneurship, innovation, and creativity.

*The Paradox Process* deals with both concepts and methods—that is, with both theory and practice. It's both a workbook and a textbook. Consequently, it tackles the subject of paradox at three levels:

1. The why of it
2. The what of it
3. The how of it

As you go along through the book, you will be invited to examine ideas about creativity, change, paradox, and innovation. Pay close attention to how these ideas can be translated into specific actions and methods that will make innovation work for you.

## THE ORIGINS OF PARADOXICAL THINKING

You'll be asked to reflect on these ideas and methods, and to test them out. This is no book for speed readers. To the contrary, read it slowly and with reflection. To help you slow down and think more, I've included speed bumps at intervals, which ask you to stop, reflect, write something down, or work on a puzzle.

This book is chiefly about contrary thinking, dialectical logic, and Janusian thinking. All three deal with the creative use of opposites, which forms the basis of paradoxical thinking.

*Contrary thinking* is a process developed by Humphrey Neill, a Vermont investment counselor, who also referred to it as "thinking in opposites." Neill's 1951 book, called *The Art of Contrary Thinking,* describes how investors can do better by doing the opposite of what the market is doing, following some rather arduous mental disciplines that constitute this form of thinking. My research further discovered that there were people in every field who engage quite consciously in contrary thinking, frequently with remarkable and impressive results. This relatively unknown Yankee investor has to be one of the great contributors to modern knowledge and the understanding of creativity, innovation, and independent thought. Neill signaled our attention and caused a consciousness of contrary thinking to swell. He invented the word *contrarian,* which has become part of our common vocabulary. Here, taken from his book, are some of Neill's thoughts on the subject of contrary thinking:

> The art of contrary thinking may be stated simply: Thrust your thoughts out of the rut. In a word, be a nonconformist when using your mind.

The art of contrary thinking consists of training your mind to ruminate in directions opposite to general public opinion; but weigh your conclusions in the light of current events and current manifestations of human behavior.

To be contrary means you have to be opposed to the obvious—and that is frequently quite baffling.

Very few people ever take the trouble to look at both sides of questions—indeed, ever take the trouble to think very much even on one side.

The purpose in using the "opposite approach" is to think through a given problem, or to gain thereby a fresh and different approach to a solution.

Try batting the ball around the next time you have a problem to solve. Toss in all the contrary angles you can think of. You will find this pro and con method most helpful in rounding out the information you require for a sound solution.

Under the Theory of Contrary Opinion, if everybody seems to be of the same mind, we contrarians opine otherwise.

*Dialectical logic,* which had been put forward in the mid-nineteenth century by German philosopher Georg Wilhelm Friedrich Hegel, takes an idea, entertains its opposite, and then attempts to fuse the two into a third idea, which becomes a new idea in its own right. The dialectical process is said to entail the three sequential steps of *thesis, antithesis,* and *synthesis.* For convenience and simplicity, I refer to dialectical logic simply as *Hegelian thinking,* particularly as I take some liberties with it, saying that it is paralogical rather than logical.

Finally, fifteen years ago, I learned about a third, extremely exciting process called *Janusian thinking.* In his book *The Emerging Goddess: The Creative Process in Art, Science, and Other Fields,* Albert Rothenberg, a professor at Harvard Medical School, describes the process of which he is the original discoverer as "actively conceiving two or more opposites or antitheses simultaneously." Professor Rothenberg named the method *Janusian thinking,* after Janus, the Roman god of doorways, whose head had two faces pointed in opposite directions.

Rothenberg reported that all major breakthroughs he had studied in the fields of art and science had been the result of this process of contemplating two or more opposites at the same time. One of his examples of Janusian thinking was the Watson and Crick discovery that DNA consists of two identical strands of molecules connected together in opposing spirals. In other words, two things could be the opposite of each other but exist together at the same time. He also explained that Nobel laureate Edwin McMillan got his idea for the synchrotron—the high-energy particle accelerator that permitted the discovery of subatomic particles—when he conceived of particles being in states of too high energy and too low energy at the same time. Among other things, Dr. Rothenberg's brilliant research opened my mind to the realization that creative people are more eager to embrace opposites than are their less creative peers.

I have classified these three ways of using opposites under the general umbrella of paradoxical thinking, on the grounds that all three involved seeing some logical contradiction that somehow made enormous sense.

As I began to delve into literature on the nature of opposites, some of which dated back to the ancient Greeks, I came to realize that paradoxical thinking worked well because *reality itself was paradoxical.* The observation that reality is constructed from the building blocks of opposites has been observed many times throughout history, yet somehow this truth has not penetrated Western society on any broad scale. This, despite the fact that Newtonian physics, relativity theory, and quantum mechanics—the three prides of modern science—consist mainly of statements about the existence and interaction of opposites.

My interest in paradox has changed me from a person who thought he inhabited a reality that was logical, rational, and reasonable to a new person who sees reality as paradoxical, irrational, and absurd. I am, of course, not the first to be profoundly changed by the discovery that all is paradox, nor am I the first to guess that this realization might help us be more creative as well as wiser.

The great magic of a paradox is that it sounds absurd, contradictory, or illogical at first glance but at second look turns out to be brilliant, true, and logical. Paradoxes open up new possibilities, break through mental walls, and pull the rug out from under false preconceptions. The power of paradox is therefore nothing short of miraculous.

## THE REST OF THE STORY

In Chapter 2, "Handling Hyperchange Through Creativity," you will examine the circular connection between change and innovation, such that the more change there is, the more innovation we need; and the more innovation there is, the more change we will get. This spiral whirls us faster and faster into a future whose shape and character are beyond imagination—and certainly beyond prediction. Thus, innovation is a strategy that every organization has to have at its core. It is no simple add-on; it must become the heart and soul of corporate existence.

Chapter 3, "Paradoxical Thinking: Examples and Methods," describes the concept of thinking in opposites in more detail, and explains the three different forms of outcomes that come from such thinking.

To repeat, one kind of paradoxical breakthrough comes from going in a direction directly opposite to convention. The second comes from putting two opposite and contradictory ideas into some novel and creative juxtaposition. The third kind of breakthrough integrates two opposite and contradictory ideas in such a thorough stage of intimacy that a wholly new entity appears; it carries the whole process of thinking in opposites and paradox to a point where the opposites seem almost to vanish into thin air. They merge to create something entirely new.

Chapter 4, "Opposites Are Everywhere," will open the doors of your mind to the idea that everything in the universe has its opposite. It will also provide examples of paradoxical innovations in every industry imaginable: transportation, chemicals, plastics, banking, insurance, medicine, and education, as well as in fields such as engineering, design, marketing, finance, and organization. You will also learn the astonishing truth that these opposites serve as the building blocks for all that exists and that all matter, all life, and all evolution and change are the product of an interplay of opposites.

In Chapter 5, "The Paradox Mind-Set," you will see how paradoxical thinking and action unfold and what conditions are crucial to them.

Chapter 6, "The Paradox Process in Action," contains numerous case examples. These examples will fortify your growing conviction that paradoxing works. It will also help you see more deeply into how it is done.

Chapter 7, "Creative Leadership in an Era of Change," deals with paradoxical ways in which leaders construct an organization that persists with the passage of time. It depicts the leader as a time traveler poised between the two temporal opposites of past and future. The true leader sees change and innovation as the way through which the future can be assured and progress brought about. The chapter includes methods for doing two opposite things—looking backward and looking forward—and shows how looking forward is best done when preceded by a backward look.

In Chapter 8, "Creative Thinking: Characteristics and Skills," you will see in detail what creative thinking is, why it is important to you, and what you can do with it. You will examine the marvelous and sometimes strange ways in which the mind searches for, finds, and fabricates new ideas and realities.

Chapter 9, "Auxiliary Thinking Tools," contains a rich assortment of creative thinking methods that can be brought to bear on the paradoxical thinking process. Each method is described in detail so you will have no trouble adapting it to your circumstances.

Chapter 10, "Some Fun: Mind Training Exercises," has a large number of mind training exercises that are fun to do and will allow you to develop an ease with opposites and paradoxes.

These exercises use oxymorons, palindromes, sayings, and humorous anecdotes. You'll get the most benefit if you work them out with a partner or in a group. My clients find it stimulating to make them a game for the family. Instructors who facilitate seminars in creative and paradoxical thinking use them in small discussion groups.

Each chapter you read will deal with one of five general topics—change, creativity, opposites, paradox, and innovation—and how that topic relates to the other four. The reason for constructing the book in this manner is that these five topics cannot be separated from each other, nor discussed except in terms of each other. They form a holistic ensemble, a unity that is indivisible. The end result is that each chapter is different from the others, but in many ways similar to them, too. By the time you finish the book, each concept will have become as familiar as the back of your hand, and you can feel confident in its use. And since the book is meant for self-training, the idea is to work your way through the material, doing the thinking and reflecting exercises as they come along. That way, you will soon achieve a high level of practical skill in paradoxing that you can make use of well into the future.

# Chapter 2

# HANDLING HYPERCHANGE THROUGH CREATIVITY

"The art of progress is to preserve order amid change and to preserve change amid order."

—Alfred North Whitehead

This is not an age of change but of hyperchange. I call it hyperchange because it is pervasive, disruptive, unpredictable, perplexing, transformative, explosive in its pace, and destined to remain permanent. This new type of change has a different taste and smell, a different sound and a different look.

It is we humans who are producing hyperchange, but it is debatable whether we are capable of exploiting it as we should. That's because it is too much of a handful. Hyperchange is not merely one kind of change but six different kinds all mixed up together and compounded:

1. Change that is gradual and slow
2. Change that is fast but linear
3. Change that is accelerating and exponential
4. Change that is abrupt, erratic, and discontinuous
5. Change that is increasingly random and unpredictable
6. Change that is radically transformative

## CHANGE AND CREATIVITY

The literature of management and business deals with the subjects of change and creativity as if they were two unconnected matters. Yet nothing is more misleading than to separate creativity from change. Creativity and change do not exist apart from each other because they have a cause-and-effect relationship.

Creativity is the chief cause of change.

Creativity—or creation—produces new things with new properties and values. Creation, whether in nature or our own constructed world, has not stopped since the beginning of time. The result may be the appearance of a new star in the firmament, a new industry in the economy, or a new product on the market.

The opportunities opened to us by creative change and innovation are so immense that they should leave us gasping at our potential good fortune. But the unintended and undesirable by-products of hyperchange are often disruptive and disorienting.

The problems produced by change will not disappear, even if we decide to stop being creative and innovative. Thousands will continue to die in vehicular accidents, others will succumb to new diseases, millions of jobs will disappear owing to new technologies. The problems produced by change are inescapable, but must be better dealt with in the future than they have been in the past. Indeed, their solutions will require enormous amounts of creative thinking and innovative actions. In 1605, at the dawn of the age of science and technology, the English philosopher Francis Bacon admonished us to remember, "He that will not apply new remedies must expect new evils, for time is the greatest innovator." Almost four hundred years later, his admonition is still valid.

Fortunately, the opportunities opened up by hyperchange will not go away, either; they will only proliferate. Our only choice is whether to simultaneously solve the problems and exploit the opportunities or to do nothing. Broad-scale solutions are needed to deal with international crime, new diseases, and global poverty. We have to develop automobiles that pollute less. Somehow, we need to reduce governmental deficits without cutting social services. On top of all that, we need billions of small-scale solutions to help us deal with the everyday problems of life in a hyperchange world. At the same time, we need to take advantage of new opportunities and possibilities.

So it is clear that creativity and change are intertwined, almost to the point of being the same thing. Anything less than all-out, aggressive creative thinking and innovative action will fail. So let's do some analysis of what hyperchange really is, what it means, and where it comes from. Only when we analyze the nature of hyperchange can we recognize how creativity can produce the solutions we need.

Change spawns diversity and opportunity. The opposite of creativity is destruction, an equally powerful cause of change. Wars, violence, hatred, natural disasters, and disease produce changes that are unwanted, horrifying, and painful. Solving the problems produced by destructive change is still another challenge requiring immense creativity.

## THE ANATOMY OF HYPERCHANGE

The laws that govern the physical universe are thought to be eternal and immutable. All other things change, but often only gradually. The mountain erodes slowly, and the ocean is in no hurry to get warmer or colder. Other changes are a bit faster. For example, the economy changes its form and structure markedly each decade. But some changes occur at an exponential rate, accelerating as time passes. For example, the world population has grown from half a billion in 1650 to nearly 6 billion in 1996; it may rise to 7 or 8 billion by 2050. The declining cost of computer power in the last thirty years is another example. Yet the accelerated nature of technological change was first noticed and discussed a good hundred years ago. So what's so different about today's rapid change? It is abrupt and *discontinuous*. Sudden breakthroughs and alterations cut off our normal continuity with the past. Atomic power appears, new organisms are produced by gene-splicing, humans are conceived in test tubes, governments operate gambling casinos, Russia breaks out into untrammeled free enterprise.

More shocking yet is that many other changes appear to be *random*. They pop up from nowhere. They are fortuitous and inexplicable, appearing to be the result of chance. AIDS, terrorist bombings of government buildings, drive-by shootings, the Iraqi invasion of Kuwait, atrocities in the former Yugoslavia—we react with, "Hey, what's happening? Where did that come from? For heaven's sake, what must we expect next?" Worse than surprise, random changes appear out of nowhere to cause fear, confusion, and disorder.

Speed, randomness, surprise—they impact in all directions. They strike deeply in the world of work, where new forms of organization, management style, operations, and employment strategies leap into being. Hyperchange has caught most of us off guard and has ruptured almost every assumption we had concerning how to survive economically. It has altered the definition of employment, describing anew what it takes to be an effective employee, professional, or manager, and has radically changed the climates of both small and large organizations. It makes us wonder where we're going. How much change can we take?

Change has carried us into a great age of capitalism, the hegemony of the market economy. No one ever described the essence of market capitalism more succinctly or unerringly than did the renowned Harvard economist Joseph Schumpeter: The essence of market capitalism is *creative destruction*. The engine is innovation. In a torrent of change and innovation, the market economy tears up everything in its path and replaces it with new things.

Change leaves a trail of rusted wrecks, abandoned buildings, environmental pollution, stressed-out people, and broken careers in its wake. But the market economy also makes it possible to produce more. It builds shiny new edifices, catapults humans into space, connects everyone via phone, video, and computer, saves lives, and provides education and opportunities for millions. The losers weep; the winners rejoice.

Hyperchange turns the phrase "the management of change" into an oxymoron. To manage means to plan, organize, and control, but hyperchange is a roiling, boiling turmoil that cannot be managed. Forget it. Instead of wasting time trying to manage hyperchange, you must do five quite different things instead:

1. Defend yourself against destructive change to the extent that you can.

2. Find creative solutions to the problems being created by change.
3. Capitalize on all the new opportunities created by change.
4. Continue to produce positive and beneficial changes.
5. Make the world a better place by capitalizing on people's ability to discover, invent, create, and innovate to the greatest extent possible.

In these five ways you can conspire to make change your ally and not your enemy. *The Paradox Process* will help you do just that.

## THE CREATIVITY POTENTIAL

New solutions are not found in libraries or encyclopedias but in the human ability to discover and create. As a result of that ability, new solutions, large and small, are constantly forthcoming, and we see and hear of them every day. The creative instinct is never dead, but there are not yet enough new solutions coming forth, nor are they as good as they could be. Moreover, every new solution does not fit every particular case.

In most instances, companies cannot rely on generic solutions. They have to create imaginative solutions of their own, solutions uniquely fitted to their own circumstances. If they don't, problems don't get solved or they miss out on opportunities that more creative companies are able to take advantage of. Dealing with the myriad challenges of change, therefore, calls for independent thinking and original, made-at-home answers rather than on borrowed recipes. This principle of independent thought applies to not-for-profit businesses as well as for-profit businesses, voluntary organizations and government agencies, police forces and fire departments, schools and universities, and ethnic and religious groups, as well as to families and individuals.

That creativity and innovation are acts of will and desire is particularly important. Some people with high levels of intelligence but weak will are not at all creative, while others of ordinary intelligence but passion and will can sometimes be exceedingly so. Creativity springs from having a different attitude toward the world. It accepts nothing as a given and everything as subject to improvement. Such people are capable of creation and invention to a degree limited only by their power of will and imagination. The belief that anything you can conceive you can bring about may not always be true, but it is perhaps closest to truth.

One of the strangest of our culture's beliefs is that creativity deals explicitly, and even exclusively, with cultural products. As a result, it is assumed that musicians, artists, and novelists live and work creatively. Some do, but most do not. The most recalcitrant group I ever worked with consisted of eighty administrators, teachers, and students at a school of art in Massachusetts, most of whom made it plain to me that they strictly opposed the idea that artists should be original, inventive, or unorthodox. If some artists wanted to be, then fine, but it wasn't going to be them. No way. The president of the school had explained that he wanted them to have a workshop in creativity so as to break through this mind-set. This discovery that artists were no more creatively inclined than anyone else set me aback. It contradicted what I believed, and what I believe most people still hold true. But it was confirmed later by the president of a school of fine arts in Canada and I now take it to be simple fact.

The popular belief that ordinary professionals, businesspeople, and working people are not creative by nature is grossly untrue. Engineers, accountants, business managers, physicians, lawyers, and such are just as frequently creative as artists and engineers are, probably no more or no less. In fact, quite a few engineers, physicians, production managers, purchasing agents, and other working professionals display habitual ingenuity and inventiveness.

The belief that creativity is limited to artists is dangerous and costly. It stops many people who work outside of the arts from using their creative abilities, since they believe they don't have any—or, if they do have such talents, that they shouldn't use them at work. This is a tragic misconception.

## THE SECRETS OF CREATIVITY

Creative thinking is different from everyday thinking—the sort we do when we buy a house or fix a flat. I had once assumed that all intelligent thinking—whether creative or otherwise—has to be logical, rational, analytical, sequential, and conscious. But I was forced to discover that creative thinking, while rational and intelligent, is also exceedingly strange.

It is strange because a good deal of it takes place within our unconscious minds—for example, when we are asleep. Often new ideas present themselves in the form of decodable metaphors or parables rather than in straightforward, literal terms. On top of this, a good deal of whatever creative thinking that does take place is erratic and disorderly. Insights and ideas often pop into existence suddenly rather than taking form slowly and gradually. Even stranger is the fact that so many groundbreaking ideas occur to people as a result of chance and accident rather than intention, and come to them while they are looking for something else. Surprisingly often, those new ideas are not the result of any thinking at all, but come simply from seeing something in a new light.

Sometimes breakthrough ideas are brazenly stolen, not from another person but from nature, as in the case of radar, which comes from bats, or the fisherman's net, which is patterned after the spiderweb. Sometimes the theft is more covert, as when an idea that has been invented for use in one field is adapted to another, entirely different application. In 1936, the circulation manager of the *Montreal Star* taught me how to get more customers by drumming them door-to-door. He used role playing, something I thought only actors did, to teach me how to sell the *Star*. Sixty years later it's not surprising I can't remember his name, but he was a young, good-looking man who wore a fedora. The sales pitch he taught me to act out produced so many new customers I had to hire my ten-year-old brother and the girl who lived upstairs to help me deliver them.

Much of what goes on during creative thinking contradicts common wisdom, which equates intelligence only with the analysis of facts and data in a systematic way. But we have to move beyond this fallacy and use our heads to do what millions of years of evolution prepared them to do. It is time to liberate human intelligence from the clutches of culture and tradition.

Over the years, students and teachers of creativity have designed procedures and methods for increasing creativity. Indeed, the list of methods is so long that there isn't room to discuss them here. But in general, some creative processes rely on metaphors and analogies; some on states of altered consciousness; some on associational devices; some on ways to see things differently and from new angles; and some on other strategies, such as deliberate dreaming.

Many of these methods are described in Chapter 9. Not only do they work, but they work surprisingly well. What makes them work is that people have innate abilities to be creative. The methods simply bring out those abilities.

There is nothing new about creation, change, and innovation, nor about the fact that we are creative creatures. But constant ingenuity and creativity are about to become the norm in the challenging new world of hyperchange. The readiness of individuals to function creatively in their work will shift from choice to requirement. Those incapable of exercising ingenuity, resourcefulness, and inventiveness are already finding that they can scarcely keep their heads above water. So anyone hoping to thrive needs to start right now to hone those creative abilities and adopt the methods for producing innovative ideas and new solutions. These methods are learnable, teachable, and usable. Let's, therefore, now look at some of the basic processes of creative and paradoxical thinking and see how some people have used them to their great advantage.

# Chapter 3

# PARADOXICAL THINKING: EXAMPLES AND METHODS

"All behavior consists of opposites. . . . Learn to see things backward, inside out, and upside down."

—Lao-tzu

The Green Tortoise bus line, operating with about a dozen old vehicles, made scheduled runs up and down the U.S. West Coast and into the interior at about half the price of Greyhound. Its owner, Gardner Kent, had given up any hope of matching the four-day speed of Gray Rabbit, his major competitor in the low-fare business. Instead, he decided to reverse the conventional strategy he had been using to compete. Rather than trying, hopelessly, to reduce the time of the trips, he decided to make them longer. A lot longer: six rather than four days. He used the extra two days to build some "fun" into the trips, such as saunas, games, and walks in the woods. In a few years, Gardner Kent's Green Tortoise buses were carrying twenty thousand passengers a year. In fact, his new strategy worked so well that Green Tortoise was subsequently able to buy Gray Rabbit. His contrarian and paradoxical thinking produced breakthrough, surprising, and dramatic results.[1]

Gardner Kent's act of thinking in opposites was the beginning,

1. Based on the story by Murray Campbell, *The Globe and Mail* (June 8, 1991). Reprinted with permission from *The Globe and Mail*.

not the end, of a creative process that provided Green Tortoise with its salvation. Within the framework of this slow-and-fun strategy, he still had plenty of creative thinking to do or else the strategy would have had no substance. But Gardner Kent had made an astonishing breakthrough that opened up a whole new future for his company. His fun-trips strategy led him into a new market, a niche opportunity made possible by the steady current of social and economic change that turned travel into a pleasure industry as much as a transportation industry. Then, by buying Gray Rabbit, he got back into the straight transportation business, but no longer had a competitor working against him. He had the best of both worlds: a fun business and a straight business. His breakthrough idea had not only solved a problem but turned it into an opportunity. On top of this, Kent changed his company and, to a degree, changed the bus industry in his market area by introducing a new type of service.

What Kent did was the result of contrarian thinking, or switching to the opposite of what is conventional. Contrarian thinking is one of three paradoxical thinking processes that can help you gain new insights and ideas. As Chapter 1 mentioned, there are auxiliary creativity methods that you can employ (see Chapters 8 and 9), but this chapter concentrates on paradoxical thinking. It describes how such thinking can be absorbed into your thought processes to magnify their power and potential. Among other things, the chapter provides a number of mind training exercises. But first let's reflect on what Gardner Kent's case tells us about creative thinking in general.

## PRINCIPLES OF CREATIVE THINKING

The result of paradoxical thinking is often a new business idea, a new scientific concept, a new design, a new product, a new service, or a new teaching method. This creative activity embodies five basic principles.

1. *Necessity is the mother of invention.* Gardner Kent and the Green Tortoise bus line reminds us of this truism. Necessity, some-

times desperation, will often lead us to ideas we would not otherwise have thought of.

2. *Persistence pays off.* Never give up hope. Keep looking. Successful breakthroughs are often the result of persistence. Occasionally, breakthroughs occur quickly, but often they don't. Don't put yourself out of the game prematurely. Thomas Edison once said, "Genius is ten percent inspiration and ninety percent perspiration."

Yet the question remains, If the answers can come at all, why can they not come more quickly? Then, when the answer does come, we say, "It's so obvious, I could kick myself." Part of the reason may be that it takes time to clear your mind of old solutions. Besides, you may know intellectually that you need a new idea, but you may not yet be emotionally ready to go after it. Emotion drives everything we do, including our thinking.

3. *Keep the faith.* Trust your ability to come up with breakthrough ideas. Your brain is the most complex entity in the universe. The cerebral cortex is constructed of 10 billion components—the neurons that receive, store, organize, and transmit information. And the average neuron interacts with thousands upon thousands of other neurons in rapidly changing patterns. When the thinking process gets going, the possibilities are limitless.

4. *Deviate from the norm.* Creative thinking is different from the thinking we do as we go about our daily routines. Under the pressure to survive, Kent's mind went off on a tangent, away from the ordinary. It was only then that he was able to come up with an idea that at first seemed illogical: Who ever heard of beating a competitor by having your buses run slower than they should?

We have been taught to put great faith in logic, reason, and practical judgment, to do things in orderly and sequential ways, and to keep our feet on the ground. Unfortunately, we pay a price for that learning. It's difficult to think the opposite—namely, that something illogical, foolish, and impractical may ultimately be the truly logical, reasonable, and practical thing to do.

5. *Progress is not always linear.* The path that takes us from a problem to its solution is not an even one. There are delays, frustrations, setbacks, and surprises. There are many aspects in the operation of a bus line that have to be carefully planned, organized,

and controlled. To thrive in this market, Gardner Kent had to live in two worlds at once: the operational world of regularity and schedule and the entrepreneurial world of irregularity and unpredictability. To be creative, he had to contradict what his experience had taught him.

## THE HISTORY OF THINKING IN OPPOSITES

People have been using opposites and paradox for creative purposes for a very long time. The lever is a prime example. Primitive humans discovered you could *raise up* a heavy object by *pushing down* on one end of a long piece of wood. And whoever invented the boomerang twenty thousand years ago (there are carbon-dated relics) must have been a paradoxical thinker, ever to have had the bizarre thought that a weapon could be made to come back to the thrower's hand. I can imagine one of his fellows saying to him, "Something that comes back when you throw it away? You must be crazy."

Window glass—which keeps the air *out* but lets light *in*—came into use in Roman times. Before that, windows were cut in the wall and could be closed with a solid cover, or with shutters to let air in but keep light out. It took the invention of glass (a Hegelian type of breakthrough) to give us a window that let light in and kept air out.

The Roman interest in paradox extended to the domain of the gods. Janus, as we know, had two faces, one for looking inward and backward and the other for looking forward and outward. Since the two faces looked in opposite directions, Janus could stand in a doorway and at the same time look into the room and out from it. He could look back at the year just gone by and forward to the year to come. January, the month that stands at the end of one year and the beginning of the next, is aptly named in his honor.

Several centuries before Christ, Aristotle invented an ingenious methodology for creating dramatic plays, which he based on a reversal of opposites. The method is so effective that it could be used more with great benefit by today's entertainment industry.

Plainly the mind's ability to grasp opposites in creative ways has been put to work repeatedly. One of its most brilliant was the invention of the electric generator by William Faraday in the 1830s. Here's how it happened.

Faraday had observed that a current of electricity passing through a wire could have the effect of causing the magnetized needle of a compass to deflect—that is, to move in a rotational direction—when the compass was located close to the wire. This discovery is the basis for his invention of the electric motor.

But if Faraday's discoveries and inventions had stopped with this, all we would have today would be electric motors run by batteries. Instead, Faraday took an additional mental leap. The fact that an electric current could cause magnets to move had made him wonder if the opposite could also happen: Could a moving magnet cause electricity to flow? Specifically, if a magnet were moved when it was held close enough to a wire, would the movement of the magnet cause a current to flow in the wire? To his delight, Faraday found that it did. This discovery was the springboard for his development of modern-day electrical generators.

One of the mysteries of all time is why minds like Faraday's seem instinctively to suspect that if one thing is true, its opposite may also be true. The evidence indicates that people with an appetite for opposites and the paradoxical play the game of life armed with some extra cards in the deck.

## SOME REMARKABLE ACHIEVEMENTS

Let's look at some more examples of paradoxical innovations. These examples will increase your familiarity with the world of paradoxical innovations and be a great source of confidence for your own efforts. Paradoxical thinking entails not only applying the methods provided in this book but also developing an interest in paradoxical innovations of all types and in the people who achieved them.

An additional purpose of some of these examples is to demonstrate that developing and enhancing a consciousness of paradox can be a deep and profound experience. Paradox opens new doors on how we see and feel about our careers, our lives, the services we provide to others, and what it means to be human.

## Swimming on the Spot

The most convenient way to swim is to have your own indoor pool, but conventional pools take great space and are costly to install and operate. Several innovators have designed extra-small home pools to solve this dilemma. Some pools are only twelve feet long. Strong pumps make the water flow through the pool, creating a current. You swim against the current with the feel of moving ahead through water. The water flow is variable, depending on how fast you want to swim. When you swim at just the right speed, you manage to hold yourself at a fixed point. A paradox is created: You are moving and not moving at the same time. You're moving relative to the water, but not to the pool.

One brand of these pools is fittingly called the Endless Pool. Tim Plummer of Endless Pools reports that they are installed in forty-eight states and eight foreign countries, including such distant places as Moscow, Malta, and Jakarta.

The perversity of the solution—its blatant contradiction of the conventional swimming pool—has a charm of its own. The pool is both alluringly absurd and determinedly logical. It can't help but make you smile to watch a swimmer strive so mightily to get nowhere. The basic concept is that of moving and not moving at the same time. Amazingly, this concept is also the basis of Einstein's special theory of relativity. Here's how it happened. Einstein visualized a person falling from the roof of a house. An object, falling alongside that person, would be moving relative to the house but would be standing still relative to the person. The object could be said to be both moving and not moving at the same time. Einstein described this thought of his as "the happiest thought I ever had in my life."

When an idea that originated in one field is applied to another field, the philosopher Donal Schon calls it *concept displacement.* The idea of moving and not moving at the same time keeps being applied to one endeavor after another. It migrated to the health club, where a person walks or runs on a treadmill but remains in the same spot. A recent version of the concept is the moving wall, equipped with knobby protrusions, that is used for indoor climbing. And it finds an opposite in the moving sidewalk in airports, which allows travelers to go from place to place while standing still. The most universal application is the escalator, of course. You don't walk up the stairs, but you get to the top anyway.

The moral of this story is that whenever you see a paradoxical idea in application, think about transferring it to your own business.

## Aluminum-Powered Cars

Aluminum is produced by the process of electrolysis. Huge currents of electricity are moved through large pots of aluminum oxide in solution. The electric current causes the oxygen and aluminum molecules in the aluminum oxide to separate. The liquid aluminum is then siphoned off and poured into large trays to harden. But Alcan's R&D scientists have been developing a reverse process, with significant success: to produce electricity from aluminum.

Plates of pure aluminum are put in a container that holds salt water. Electrolytic action is automatically set into motion, which generates electricity, and that electricity can be used to run motors. Batteries based on this concept have proved capable of moving light vehicles (made of aluminum, naturally) at reasonable speeds for distances of some miles. What this development work will lead to is not yet known, but do not be surprised if someday your fuel-economical car is not only made of aluminum but also runs on aluminum. As this battery operates, the aluminum plates are slowly dissolved. Do you suppose that when you run out of fuel, you will just tear off a fender?

Breakthroughs of a paradoxical character show up in every field. They come from individuals and teams who are bold enough to think in opposites and brave enough to experiment with contradictory ideas.

## A Depolluting Automobile

In 1995, *The New York Times* reported a promising automotive innovation, produced through paradoxical thinking.[2] John Novak, a salesman and commercial director of automotive emissions at the Englehard Corporation, envisaged a system called Premair. Air through

---

2. From the story by Kirk Johnson, *The New York Times* (May 28, 1995). Copyright © 1995 by The New York Times Company. Reprinted by permission.

a car radiator is coated with a catalyst that breaks ozone molecules (the main component of smog) into oxygen and changes carbon monoxide into carbon dioxide. Ford Motor Company joined with Englehard to develop applications of Novak's idea. Dr. Haren S. Gandhi, director of chemical engineering at Ford, said, "I've been in the field for twenty-eight years, and this is a completely new way of thinking. It's a new mind-set."

Mr. Novak's flash of inspiration came to him while he was working as a member of a multidepartmental team. As a member, he had been drawn into thinking about problems and opportunities that were outside his normal jurisdictional boundaries of sales and commercial matters. It is an excellent example of how it may be easier—sometimes easier for the outsider than for the insider—to think in ways that contradict existing beliefs, assumptions, and expectations. Among other things, groups are more forgiving of absurd ideas that come from amateurs who know better than from professionals and experts who can have no excuse for thinking inane thoughts. The Premair breakthrough is an encouragement to make creativity and innovations teams multidisciplinary.

## Reverse Duty-Free

Many of our global competitors are already into paradoxical thinking. Everyone knows that a duty-free shop is where you buy goods before getting on the plane to go home. But not people in the Philippines. There you buy them after getting off.

Buying after arrival in the Philippines makes possible the purchase of large gifts for friends and relatives—such objects as motorcycles, washing machines, brass beds, and even farm equipment. No small carry-on items in that list! These goods are bought by visiting Filipinos, among the 4 million of whom work overseas. As *The New York Times* put it, "A strange new permutation of duty-free shopping has catapulted an unlikely candidate, the Philippines, into the top ranks of the world's duty-free merchandisers."[3]

This reverse on the usual has made the Duty Free Philippines agency the fourth largest seller worldwide in the duty-free industry.

3. From the story by Bruce Lambert, *The New York Times* (June 24, 1995). Copyright © 1995 by The New York Times Company. Reprinted by permission.

In fact, its duty-free shops are said to rank as the third largest retailer in the Philippines. The orthodox duty-free concept may make sense in most cases, but here is an instance where the opposite is true.

The Philippines example piles up the evidence that no matter what the rest of the world is doing, you may gain enormous advantage by doing the opposite. Avoid the danger of one-sided thinking that assumes what is best in most cases is best in all cases. Sometimes the opposite is better.

## Down Under

Paradoxical solutions sometimes provoke a smile, a chuckle, or a laugh. This one will. It concerns buses, managers, and union leaders in Australia.

In healthy union-management situations, union and management enjoy a relationship that is essentially cooperative during those long periods that prevail between contract negotiations. But in contract negotiations the relationship is competitive and each party tries to win the most it can for its own side. It is a game of strategy and wits, and union leaders are capable of paradoxical thinking, too.

In Australia, public service unions have the same difficulties with strikes that public service unions have everywhere: The public can get very angry with workers. When the public is angry, the employer's hand is strengthened. It happened that bus drivers in Melbourne were thinking of going on strike, but were worried about public reaction. So what the union did instead was invent an antithetical form of strike, which they call a "positive" strike. They refused to collect fares. They went on strike while staying on the job! This defused the public's fear of inconvenience and any possible danger. It also amused them no end, making them feel grateful to the union. Everyone loves to see authority figures embarrassed. The public was less grateful, of course, after the union won and the fares went up.

There seems to be some similarity between the surprise of humor and the surprise of a paradox. Or perhaps it's because humor and paradox both put a new twist on the familiar. Joe in Boston thinks it odd that John in Sydney stands upright with his head pointing in the opposite direction. Or that someone in Sydney can call him by phone on Saturday and reach him at home in Boston on

Friday, the previous day. When Lewis Carroll wrote *Alice's Adventures in Wonderland* and *Through the Looking Glass,* he was trying to tell all of us how strange the real world actually is.

## Role Reversal

When I was at York University in Toronto, I put my undergraduate students in charge of their final course in management. They would have an opportunity to learn management by managing the course. After all, if the best way to learn something is by doing it, the best way to learn management is by managing.

The student's empowerment was to be complete. No halfway stuff. They were to design the course, operate the course, prepare the exams, and do the grading. I had in mind a completely new system of education, a true Hegelian synthesis that would put the professor and the students in radical juxtaposition. The idea was that the new system would result in qualitative and quantitative leaps in learning.

I became their educational and management consultant. Nothing more. They became the self-directed managers of a learning process and program that they would have to invent. I would attend the classroom sessions or other learning activities, but only as an observer. I would consult with them without limit, when requested. On the other hand, anytime they wanted me to do any teaching, I would do so. In fact, my unwritten contract with the university would not allow me to refuse.

From day one, the class looked, felt, and tasted different. There was a great deal of action; the tenor was energetic and busy.

The students used business games. They videotaped one of the case discussions, and viewed it as a way of studying group dynamics. They invited other instructors, corporate executives, and management consultants from the community to come in and address them. I performed the traditional teacher function in only two sessions, and of course only at the students' invitation.

The upshot? The students planned, designed, organized, and ran a course that was educationally successful beyond my (and their) expectations. At times the program seemed like a roller coaster ride. The students were charged up. The different task forces got into conflict. One student lived in fear that if other universities heard of the course, they would refuse to accept it as a credit. There was one punch thrown, and once there were tears shed. I had taken a bigger risk than I had imagined, and I wondered if the university authorities might not come down on my head if they heard what was happening. When the year ended, the students and I were both elated and relieved. We were elated with success and relieved that the continuing stress of the experiment had come to an end. The grades were written down in the form the university required, and I signed the document.

The students had not only learned *about* management, but also *how* to manage. They left with self-confidence, knowing how to formulate aims and objectives, how to plan and organize a complex undertaking, how to work individually and in teams, how to evaluate performance and improve it, and how to make important decisions and accept responsibility. They not only had managed something important but had reflected upon the experience, learned from it, and taken it away with them. Meanwhile, I learned that even though the students had learned a lot, they had been pretty good managers to start with. I reconfirmed my belief that the best way to learn anything is by doing it, not by talking about it.

I also learned that when you think about doing something that is the opposite of what is normally done, there is no way of knowing where you are going to end up. You are traveling in uncharted territory, and you'd better be ready to roll with the punches. I also learned that by bringing opposites (me and the students) together in a new way, the new blend truly is more than and different from the sum of the parts. Most of all, I learned how much of an adventure a job can become if you are willing to experiment with opposites.

## Try to Make More Mistakes

To what extent can we afford to turn our most basic beliefs on their heads? At what point does challenging common sense and reason become insanity? This is not an easy question to answer.

If paradoxing goes too far, we can disturb and frighten others—even ourselves. At a certain point, those who challenge the obvious are thought to be insane and dangerous. After all, history is full of dissenters who were put to death. Let's test the issue.

One of the most obvious, commonsense, and deeply held beliefs—one that almost everyone holds as self-evident—is that it is better to do things right rather than wrong, and to avoid making mistakes. Anyone who advocates the opposite belief—that making mistakes is good and people should be encouraged to make more of them—might properly be regarded as a fool and a dangerous person to have around.

But there is a good argument in favor of mistakes. People whose guiding rule in life is to avoid making mistakes never get into trouble. But to avoid making mistakes, you never do anything. The second best way is to do little. Consequently, people who are very mistake-averse do little and achieve little. Their biggest mistake is not making mistakes!

Another way of not making mistakes is to never do anything new or different. When you do anything new, the chances are you'll make a mistake. So stick to what is well established. Tell yourself, "If it ain't broke, don't fix it" and "Leave well enough alone." Try to follow only the "best practices." Nothing new is tried, nothing new gets done.

All societies teach children the right things to do, reward them for doing so, and penalize them for not. Schools grade students on their ability to provide the correct answers and penalize them for making mistakes. Small wonder that so many people grow up to be error averse and to zealously avoid making mistakes. *They learn to be perfect rather than productive.*

If social controls worked perfectly and we never did anything wrong, there'd be no change or innovation. Fortunately, they don't work perfectly. Some members of society defy those controls and take chances, think new thoughts, do new things, make mistakes, and learn from their mistakes.

The truth is that to live fully means being prepared and willing to make mistakes. We say, "Live and learn," with the implication that being human means learning and growing. Business has a permanent need to have people who can take the initiative, act, make mistakes, and learn. Is it possible that some companies are so intent on being error free and having no one make mistakes that they do grave damage to themselves?

Fortunately some business leaders avoid the mistake of making their enterprises mistake free. Borg-Warner's chairman, James Bere, states, "Most people do not want to take the risk of failure, and therefore they do not want their people to make mistakes. And I say it's the absolute reverse. You do not develop a quality person without making mistakes."

In an age when entrepreneurship and innovation are the only assurance of a viable future, how do we teach people how to make mistakes? This is what teachers and trainers have to do when teaching and training are for entrepreneurship and innovation. His students' fear of making mistakes was the problem that Professor Jack Matson of the University of Michigan had to overcome in training student entrepreneurs to be creative. Matson teaches entrepreneurship to second-year MBA students. Students in his course must start up a business and have customers before the end of the fourteen-week period. Naturally many of the first ideas of the students fail and they have to come up with others until they find one that works.

Professor Matson himself experienced many failures in his attempt to find ways of teaching creativity. By accident he discovered that students who tried a variety of things in a trial-and-error process were more successful than those who went straight for one idea. He coined the phrase "intelligent fast failure" to describe their approach, meaning they learned from their mistakes.

Finding that students abandoned creative attempts when grades were at stake, Dr. Matson reversed the usual grading approach and awarded the highest grades to students who failed the most—that is, who "risked the most." His one proviso was that the failed attempts show signs of intelligence and thoughtfulness. The main challenge, he found, was helping students learn the benefits of failure. He explains, "In the first part of the course, the students had to produce the worst consumer product and write a résumé that guaranteed not to make them employable. One day they had to dress for failure. The results were amazing. All the students participated with fanatical creative energy. Grade reversal worked. They saw creative talent within themselves. So what if they produced the worst item or looked the lousiest, they began to recognize their abilities to be innovative."[4]

No one wants an airline pilot or a cardiac surgeon to make mistakes. There are times and places where mistakes are fatal. Like-

4. Jack Matson, "Failure 101: Rewarding Failure in the Classroom to Stimulate Creative Behavior, *Journal of Creative Behavior,* 25, no. 1 (1991). By permission of the copyright holder, The Creative Education Foundation, 1050 Union Road, Buffalo, NY 14224.

wise, when a product is being made or a service is being delivered, there is no time for making mistakes.

The time to make mistakes is when something new is being created or when action has to be taken in the face of uncertainty. In the new world of corporate innovation and entrepreneurship, you need to become expert at knowing when to make mistakes and when not to. And you need to know that increasing your efforts to be creative will mean making more mistakes. When you encourage your employees to be more creative and innovative, tell them that you expect them to make mistakes, and hope that they do.

## UNDERSTANDING PARADOXES

The word *paradox* comes from two Greek words, *para* and *doxa,* and originally meant something contrary to received opinion or expectation. At first glance a paradox appears bizarre or absurd, or at best enigmatic. It contradicts common sense and logic, flies in the face of all reason, and yet is strangely compelling. Someone defined a paradox as a truth standing on its head. But at second glance, a paradox is brilliantly true, valid, and sensible. Solutions that arise out of paradoxes provide initial surprise, followed by delight, as preconceptions are broken through. Their word *paradox* came eventually to have a special connotation to the Greeks of something incredible and marvelous. That is the same attitude that you will find developing yourself as you discover how exciting and useful paradoxical thinking can be.

Most people are not yet attuned to the reality of opposites and their importance. But society's pathfinders, innovators, and leaders are tuning in. You can join in that process, particularly if you have hospitable feelings toward the opposite sides of ideas. You can take creative advantage of paradoxical solutions through manipulation, rearrangement, or integration.

Paradoxical thinkers take it as axiomatic that there are two sides, two opposites to everything, and that both sides have their plusses and minuses, their positives and negatives. They are capable of looking at both sides coolly and dispassionately and of giving each side its due. In addition, they have the intellectual courage to question conventional wisdom, as well as the drive and mental energy to construct new ideas and images.

How do some people come about their consciousness of opposites? Here are two different cases of persons who came to their awareness in different ways.

## Discovering the Law of Opposites

Hugh Aaron is the former CEO and owner of a plastics company in Belfast, Maine. When I asked where he had heard about the art of thinking in opposites, his answer was "nowhere." Then he went on to explain.

At one time, he found himself bothered by an employee problem. Employees temporarily laid off because of sales came back to work bitter, insecure, and less committed—a condition of mind no better for themselves than for the company. How could he operate without having to have layoffs?

In an article he wrote for *The Wall Street Journal,* he said, "We often broke loose from the bounds of conventional thinking by seeking the solution in a condition precisely opposite the one troubling us. We call this our 'lesson of the opposites.' We used it here. Since laying off is the problem, then perhaps working overtime, its opposite, is the answer."[5]

Aaron decided that if the company could somehow manage not to hire new employees when business increased, those people would not be there to be laid off when business subsided. It would mean that employees might have to work a wearying amount of overtime, but the reward would be no layoffs. The employees agreed to this proposal, and the result was a new era in which the company held to a promise of zero layoffs.

The benefits from the innovation were too numerous to be listed. According to Aaron, "employee morale attained a new height; turnover, already low, became negligible. Pride in being part of a caring organization was clearly evident. A desire to exert extra effort on behalf of the company became the norm."[6]

5. Hugh Aaron, "Recession Proofing a Company's Employees. *The Wall Street Journal* (April 3, 1995). Reprinted with permission of *The Wall Street Journal* © 1995 Dow Jones & Company, Inc. All rights reserved.
6. Ibid.

## Paradox in Paper

Joldine Lee is an independent thinker. Her design creations are in the field of paper products, including envelopes manufactured from used office paper. She folds discarded business letters into envelopes so that the unused side is on the outside, with the typing on the inside where anyone curious to read it can do so.

Customers find the idea amusing, and the business thrives. Unlike conventional recycling, which involves complex physical and chemical processes, nothing needs to be done to her still perfectly good, even if half used, paper.

Lee is an architect by profession, an expert at working in three-dimensional space and taking the environment into account. When she was a student, one day her professor handed out three quotes from famous authors and asked her to choose one of them as the inspiration for a project. The one Lee chose came from the philosopher Heidegger and dealt with the subject of opposites. This started her on an architectural career in which opposites would be her theme. From that point on, all her school projects dealt with opposites.

For her final-year thesis, Lee designed a community building for Yellowknife, in Canada's Northwest Territories. In summer in Yellowknife, it is light all day and the town atmosphere is lively. In winter, it is dark all day and the town is somber. Her idea was to design a building that related to this dualism, one that opened out in the summer and closed in the winter. Also, it would be a building to serve the large summer transient population as well as the winter residents. The outside of the building would equal the inside in size and quality, with the outside perimetered with an attractive glass wall and equipped with tentlike coverings and awnings. How did Lee get to be a paradoxer? Partly because her mother encouraged her to question things.

## THE THREE CLASSES OF PARADOXICAL THINKING

Now that you have looked at a number of innovations produced by paradoxical thinking, it is useful once again to sort out the different kinds of paradoxical thinking. Each is distinct, but all entail the mental manipulation of opposites.

## Contrary Thinking

You use contrary thinking when: (1) you conceive of doing something opposite; (2) you think of replacing something by its opposite, whether that thing is a belief, a value, an idea, or an object; (3) you entertain the thought that your opponent is right and you are wrong, or just assume that an opposite point of view might be worth looking at.

We are mentally programmed by our upbringing and social environment to believe that whatever is common and traditional is right and that whatever differs from it is wrong. This programming is so effective that we don't know it exists. Contrary ideas make us feel uncomfortable and we draw back. As an example, test your feelings as you contemplate the following contrarian images: a black wedding gown, a white tuxedo, black writing paper, a black ceiling, an ugly TV announcer, a wealthy beggar, a skinny wrestler, a humble dictator, a tall pigmy.

Contrarian thinking involves questioning a common belief or practice, then looking at what its reverse is. If the opposite makes sense, go in that opposite direction. Do the reverse of what is normally done—insult instead of flatter the audience, have the students teach the teachers, put the living room at the back of the house, serve the soup at the end of the meal—all in a creative, practical, and imaginative way and with a purpose in mind, such as a problem to be solved or an opportunity to be exploited.

## Janusian Thinking

As construed for our purposes, Janusian thinking involves conceptualizing or bringing two opposites together in your mind, holding them there together at the same time, considering their relationships, similarities, pros and cons, and interplay, then creating something new and useful. This two-sided thinking is quite difficult because it requires holding two opposites together in your mind, a mental feat. The great Gestalt psychologist Fritz Perls once said, "The ability to achieve and maintain an interested impartiality between imagined opposites, however absurd one side may seem, is essential for any new creative solution of problems." Perls' statement is so important that I have memorized it. Someday I am going to have it framed and put on my office wall, so I am reminded of it every day. It is the most important single thing I have ever read on the subject of what is required to do paradoxical thinking. Try to keep Perls' dictum in mind all the way through the rest of this book. I will repeat it once again later in this book. It's too important to mention only once.

Some illustrations of Janusian thinking are: a black and white checkerboard; black and white keys on a piano, white shoelaces on black shoes, black shoelaces on white shoes, a white shirt with a black tie, a black shirt with a white tie, white ink on black paper, black ink on white paper. A physical example of a Janusian construct is a knife, which has a sharp blade that will cut your hand and a handle that will not. When separate, the opposite parts are not useful for slicing beef, but joined together they synergize, producing a remarkably proficient tool.

## Hegelian Thinking

When you visualize how to fuse, combine, mingle, integrate, or synthesize two opposites to produce a third entity, you are engaging in Hegelian thinking. The thing produced may be an object, a product, a service, an idea, a goal, a method, a musical form, an art form. Examples are newspaper photographs, which consist of a pattern of black dots on white paper yet magically produce a face; the male and female parts that make a hose coupler; and the black dots on a white background that we see below, arranged in such a way as to produce not merely a number of dots but a triangle, which is something above and beyond the dots themselves.

An entity can have its unique character and properties, distinct from the parts that make it up. For example, water's properties differ from the properties of oxygen and hydrogen, of which it is made. The science philosopher Arthur Koestler referred to these wholes as *holons* to highlight the fact that properties of the whole are different from and more than the sum of the parts. At a certain point when black and white are blended, they cease being either black or white and become a new and different color, an unambiguous gray. At a certain point of experience and skill a fusion can take place between a living pilot and a lifeless airplane so much that the plane seems alive and the pilot feels part of that plane. There is, therefore, a transcendent unity that emerges from the marriage of opposites. It was Hegel's view that every thought or thing produces its opposite, and then unites with it to form a single new, holistic entity. Yet that new entity will in turn evoke its own opposite, or antithesis, thus starting the whole process again, forever.

Change and evolution never stop, in nature and in society. The sequence of events passes through three stages: thesis, antithesis, and synthesis. Thus the Hegelian paradigm provides, at one stroke, a portrait of both transformative change and transformative creativity.

## TRYING OUT THE ART OF PARADOXICAL THINKING

People's minds run in their own particular tracks and are drawn to certain interests without their knowing why. I'm interested in mechanical gadgets, for example. When I first became fascinated by the theory of paradoxical innovation, I thought I might test my abilities by inventing a paradoxical hammer that could both drive nails in and not drive nails in at one and the same stroke. I had no use in mind for such a hammer and had absolutely no idea what a paradoxical hammer might be like.

The household hammer is already a paradox, of Janusian nature. It can both pound in nails and pull them out. The original hammer, pure and simple, did not do this; it only drove nails in. Its opposite was the nail puller, an invention made necessary when people hammered nails in and wanted to pull them out. The relatively recent invention of today's claw hammer was the result of Janusian thinking. Someone visualized how to put a hammer and a nail puller in workable juxtaposition on a single handle.

But what I was after was a new kind of hammer, one that would be a Hegelian synthesis. For three aggravating days I got nowhere, but in the middle of the third night I sat bolt upright in bed. Below is a picture of my dialectical hammer. If a nail is struck with it, the nail will go in, but not all the way because of its countersunk head.

At breakfast, I bragged about my success while admitting that it was a pretty useless tool. My daughter was consoling. She told me it could be used to put nails into a wall for hanging pictures, since they would protrude just the right amount. I was not consoled. Weeks later at a seminar, I told the story as a kind of joke on myself. However, one manager pointed out that I should have tried to invent a paradoxical nail instead. Unfortunately, he went on to explain, paradoxical nails had already been invented. Billions of them were used annually.

The paradoxical nail is used in construction as a means of nailing things together temporarily. It consists of a nail with two heads, one above the other. The upper head is struck by the hammer and drives the nail in, but the lower head stops the nail from going in all the way. The patent on this nail would have run out by now, but one point is clear. It is quite possible for anyone using paradoxical thinking to invent a product that can be lucrative. I made the mistake of inventing the wrong product.

My hammer story is also an example of how not to do it. There was no purpose or objective in my inventing a new hammer. A better demonstration of the paradoxical process might have been to come up with a new way to market my seminars or consulting services. Still, it proved that I could make Hegelian thinking work.

## Explore the Nature of Opposites

The following test will help you to experience some sensory opposites, and have a bit of fun at the same time.

Get four large bowls. Put hot water in the left one, tepid water in the middle two, and cold water in the right one. Put your left hand in the hot water and your right hand in the cold water, and hold your hands in the water until they feel normal and have adjusted to the heat or the cold. Now put each hand into one of the center bowls. The water will feel cool to your left hand and warm to your right hand. Two things that are identical will appear to be opposite each other.

To experience hot and cold paradoxes at their ultimate, my management consultant neighbor John Prior suggests a sauna party in the winter in Scandinavia. After you get your body temperature raised in the sauna, you run down to the lake barefooted through the snow. The snow melts on your feet and freezes as you run, yet you feel a pleasant coolness. As you run to the lake, your skin cools down a great deal but you don't feel that happening. When you jump into the icy cold water of the lake, you feel a sudden warmth rather than cold. The reason is that lake water, cold as it is, is still warmer than the outside air.

Similar experiences have moved John to the conclusion that how you see things, including opposites, is relative to your state of body and mind. Consequently, by deliberately altering your attitude or your angle of view, you can see opposites in new and different ways. These changed or altered perspectives will open you to new insights and realizations of a creative nature.

## Return to Childhood Habits

This book is an invitation to you to return to some of the fascination with opposites you enjoyed as a child, but pursue them now with a great deal more profundity and scope.

When you were in your terrible twos you found it quite gratifying to do the opposite of whatever your parents wanted you to do. In fact, your parents may have learned to ask you to do the opposite of what they really wanted you to do. When you were a few years older, you still had an inclination to explore and test the opposite of whatever everyone else was doing. For example, you probably experimented with looking at the world upside down and backward by bending down and putting your head between your legs. You tried walking on your hands instead of your feet. You learned how to walk on the top of board fences instead of beside them. You drew faces that still looked like faces when you viewed them upside down, as does the sketch of a woman shown below. You spelled your name backwards, just to see what it looked like. I still remember that mine came out as Tomred Terrab.

Doing paradoxical thinking as an adult means renewing your interest in opposites, this time for commercial, intellectual, artistic, or practical reasons.

For example, one of the great skills of the paradoxical thinker is the ability to quickly visualize the opposite of anything and then move back and forth from one thing to its opposite and back again as often as wanted. One of the best ways to develop your skill with opposites is by practicing on the reversible images in the exercises that follow.

There is not much to be gained by doing the reversals only once. Go through all the images in succession, reversing each one. Then go back to the beginning and do them all again, following the instructions of reversing each one a number of times before moving on to the next one. These repetitive exercises will resurrect some of your childhood reversal skills and get your brain reacclimatized.

### EXERCISE 1: THE NECKER CUBE

To be creative, you must make yourself see things from different perspectives. The Necker cube, shown below, is a classic diagram for studying cognitive skills. Here you will use it to enhance your contrarian and paradoxical aptitudes. Stare at it and then move your eyes away. Then stare at it again. You will find that it flips its tilt and direction. At one moment it is tilted upward, then it tilts downward. After a while, you will find that it tilts in whichever of the two directions you wish—that is, you will be seeing what you want to see. This exercise shows how your mind can manipulate your perceptions. Make a copy of the diagram, keep it on your desk, and practice with it for a few days, seeing how fast you can get it to flip back and forth. You will be making your brain more flexible and quick moving.

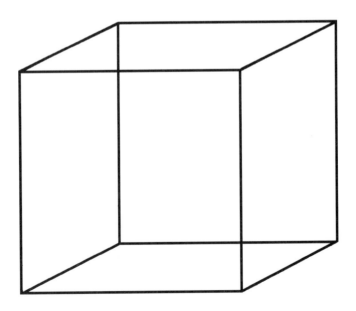

## EXERCISE 2: THE VIRTUAL NECKER CUBE

Following is an illusory Necker cube, to be done in the same manner as the previous exercise. It may have a better training effect because of its greater complexity.

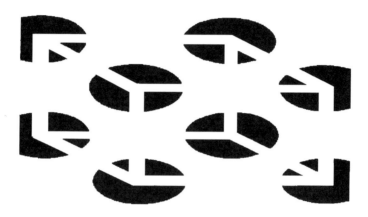

## EXERCISE 3: THE THREE CUBES

The following diagram always has an enormous impact on business groups. Chuck Chambers, the CEO of Sara Lee Direct in Winston-Salem, North Carolina, was so taken by it that he had mugs and sweatshirts made up with it in two colors to be handed out at workshops where creative thinking skills were being taught. This exercise has two goals. The first is to reverse the cube so that at one time you see two cubes on the bottom and one on the top, and then two cubes on the top and one on the bottom. The second goal is to see three cubes on the bottom and one on top, and then three on top and one on the bottom. (The third cube is visible in the middle, between two cubes, but it sticks out at an angle either upward or downward.) The latter is initially quite difficult to see, but once seen is obvious. If after trying for a while you find you still can't see this middle cube, ask other people to point it out to you.

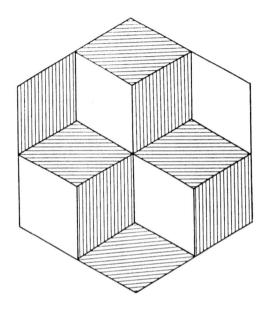

## EXERCISE 4: THE BLOCK AND THE CORNER

This exercise can be a bit difficult. Below, you can see either a room with a block filling up half the corner, or else see a large solid block with a smaller block stuck to it on the outside. Or you can see the same large block with a small block cut out in it. Work at it, and it will come; if you have trouble ask a friend to help. Play with this picture for a good while until you get it to behave as you want it to behave.

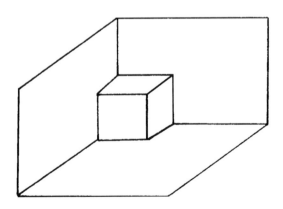

## EXERCISE 5: THE STAIRS

This exercise is straightforward: Below, you see either normal stairs ascending to the right or upside down stairs descending from the left. Try to see both possibilities.

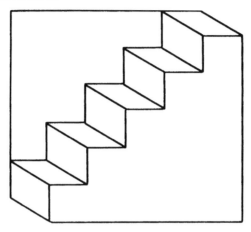

## EXERCISE 6: THE FOLDED PAPER

This exercise is a bit odd. Either you see a screen that is folded toward you and upright, or a screen that is folded away from you but lying down. Again, work at it until you see both possibilities.

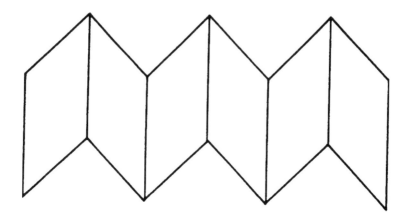

### EXERCISE 7: THE RINGS

Here, you seem to be either looking left through the rings or looking right. Keep at it until you see them both ways.

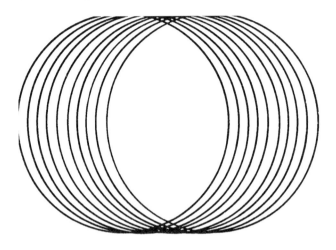

### EXERCISE 8: VASE AND FACES

This is the classic in perception literature. Using a reversible figure of this type, Albert Rothenberg found that people who were rated high on creativity by their colleagues at work reversed these figures faster than those who were rated lower. See how rapidly you can make the switch.

## Exercise 9: The Old Woman/Young Woman Drawing

You can see either an old woman or a young woman, both looking to the right, in the next figure. Do the usual mental exercise of reversing these two opposites. The old woman has a huge nose and sunken mouth, her chin is buried in the fur of her coat, and she has a scarf over her head. The nose of the old woman is the whole of the young woman's face, which is tilted away from you with only her right eyelid and the tip of her nose visible. The old lady's eye is the young woman's nose.

This picture dates back to the 1920s, when psychologists were studying the effects of preconceptions on what people see and perceive in a sit-

uation. The picture is actually a composite—a synthesis if you will—of two separate pictures. When experimental subjects were shown pictures of the old woman, before being shown the composite, they could see only the old woman when they were shown the composite. The contrary was also true with subjects first exposed to the picture of the young woman. If preconceptions can be so persuasive with such a simple thing as a picture, imagine the effects of our perceptions when governed by preconceptions and beliefs instilled in us over decades. It helps explain why taking a contrary view requires fortitude of mind.

Another interesting feature of this drawing is that the artist who created it accidentally drew in a number of other figures, some of which are easier to see than others. For example, the piece of fur to the right of the old woman's fur can be seen as a porcupine. If you see the other part of the fur as the left shoulder of a gorilla, the gorilla appears to be writing with a crayon on a blackboard. Again, the lower right part of the old lady's scarf—the part that touches her face and extends up beside her hair—can be seen as a penguin with its head tilted up to the right. There are several other things detectable in the drawing, if you want to look hard enough. In fact, there are at least five more figures that my workshop participants have found, and I doubt they have seen them all.

Curiously, once most seminar participants find the old woman and the young woman, they look no further. But some do look again, and they are the ones who bring these other figures to my attention. My suspicion is that those who keep looking have a better track record in entrepreneurship.

### EXERCISE 10: THE BIRD

This is a straightforward exercise. The bird can be seen flying in either an easterly or a westerly direction. You should be able to see both. As a bonus, you can even see a third bird flying southeast.

### EXERCISE 11: AMBIGRAMS

The next several figures are what are called *ambigrams*.[7] Ambigrams are the invention of John Langdon, of the College of Design Arts at Drexel University in Philadelphia. Not only are these words in the ambigrams reversible, they are all words that in themselves have to do with opposites. Most require you to turn the page upside down; when you do, the

7. From John Langdon, *Wordplay* (New York: Harcourt Brace Jovanovich, 1992). Out of print, but still available from John Langdon at fax number (215) 569-8889.

word will stay the same. In each case below, look straight on at the ambigram and follow the procedure explained.

The large black *O* can be seen to contain a white *I*. See it as an *O* and you read *flop*. See it as an *I*, and you can read *flip*. So what we've got is an ambigram that *flip/flop*s. Since mental flip-flopping is part of what we do in paradoxical thinking, this ambigram could make a good sweatshirt logo for an innovation team or a diagram on office coffee cups as a reminder that paradoxical thinking is a good way to get new ideas.

Turn the page upside down to see this classically neat and perfect ambigram do its trick for you.

# reversal

To get this one, do a reversal of your usual way of looking at words and turn the page upside down for this one, too.

# contrarycontrarycon

Doing the contrary of what everyone else does will often lead to a problem's solution. Be contrary, contrary, contrary, contrary all the time, and you will be sure to annoy some people. But you'll be surprised at how often you are the person who delivers the winning ideas. Once again, turn the page upside down.

# polarized

Opposites often take the form of polarized extremes, like black and white, high and low, tall and short. But in reality there are always the in-betweens, the grays, the average, the blands. In-between and average are comfortable but not creative. It is the polarized extremes from which we can often best create new things. Sharp blacks and whites give you the vivid design of the checkerboard; really high gives you the soaring skyscraper, really low, the useful pup tent; really tall gives you the star basketball player, really small, the winning jockey. Once again turn the page upside down.

And finally, a synthesis is what you get when you use Hegelian thinking to merge two opposites. The opposite of synthesis is analysis. It's too bad that when this ambigram is turned upside down it doesn't read analysis. Oh, well.

### EXERCISE 12: PROBLEM SOLVING

The previous exercises have been practice in seeing and perceiving opposites. What now follows are a few problems whose purpose is to use your ability to see opposites as a means for reaching solutions. Granted, these are not real problems, but they do require the same skills. See the answers at the end.

| A |   |   |   | E | F |   | H | I |   | K | L | M | N |   |   |   |   |   | T |   | V | W | X | Y |   |
|---|---|---|---|---|---|---|---|---|---|---|---|---|---|---|---|---|---|---|---|---|---|---|---|---|---|
|   | B | C | D |   |   | G |   |   | J |   |   |   |   | O | P | Q | R | S |   | U |   |   |   |   |   |

Where does the *Z* go?

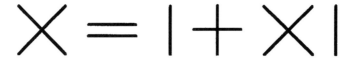

The above equation appears to be incorrect. Your problem is to make it look right to you but without touching it with pen or pencil. Other than that, you can do anything you want with it.

There is a definite pattern to this arrangement of designs. What's the next figure in the sequence?

**Answers:**

The answer to the first problem is at the top because the letters are all straight-line in shape, and the ones at the bottom are all curved. The answer to the second is to turn the sheet upside down, or read the equation from left to right. The answer to the third problem is a double 8 because the last figure was two sevens joined face-to-face, one of which was printed backwards; the previous figure was two sixes joined together, one of which was facing backwards; before that were two fives, and so on until the first figure is two ones, one of which is reversed, joined face-to-face.

## SUMMARY

It should be clear that many important breakthroughs and innovations have a paradoxical character, and have been the result of paradoxical thinking. So, being able to think in opposites is essential for intelligent thought, including creative thought. There are three forms of paradoxical thinking, namely contrary thinking, Janusian thinking, and Hegelian thinking. When you are able to identify these three forms of paradoxical thinking, you can put them to use, developing your ability and willingness to see, perceive, think, and imagine in terms of opposites. Like all human abilities, paradoxical thinking is a skill that you can develop and sharpen through training and use.

The next chapter, "Opposites Are Everywhere," will heighten your consciousness of the degree to which everything is constructed of opposites, that everywhere will be opposites, and that breakthroughs are the product of paradoxical thinking.

# Chapter 4

# OPPOSITES ARE EVERYWHERE

"Clay is molded into vessels,
And because of the space where nothing exists we are
able to use them as vessels.
Doors and windows are cut out in the walls of a house,
And because they are empty spaces, we are able to use
them.
Therefore, on the one hand we have the benefit of
existence,
And the other of non-existence."

—Lao-tzu

There is scarcely anything in the world as omnipresent as the existence of opposites. Yet there is probably nothing we spend less time thinking about. Because opposites are in the background, we don't see them with the vividness we should. But to be creative and innovative, you have to pull opposites out of the background and put them in the foreground, where they will stand out and be visible.

It is often said that a fish does not know that water exists because the fish takes it for granted. Water surrounds him, touches him, and is taken in and out of his body. The result is that he's oblivious to it. When it comes to opposites, we are like fish. Opposites are so much around us, and so much part of us, that we don't see them. This chapter will help you look at opposites more fully and attentively.

Our understanding of opposites needs to become more analytical and imaginative. If we don't handle opposites well, in a clear-headed way, we will pay a price, but if we handle them analytically and imaginatively we will reap a profit. The more you look at opposites, the more fascinated you will become with them. They have their own special magic, which has made them irresistible to thousands of inventors, innovators, entrepreneurs, and leaders.

## OPPOSITES ARE THE BUILDING BLOCKS OF REALITY

The world, and any single thing in it, could not exist without opposites. This is the trump card that paradoxers throw down on the table. It is the rock of their belief. Opposites are the building blocks of reality. To support this assertion, the paradoxer has to do nothing more than call on the evidence from modern physics.

Matter and energy are composed of opposites. For example, hydrogen, the simplest element of matter that exists, consists of one proton and one electron. Proton and electron are bits of energy, one negatively charged and one positively charged. The electrons, which have a negative charge, orbit around the proton of the atom, which has a positive charge. They are held together by the balance that exists between the electromagnetic force that pulls them together and other opposing effects that keep them apart.

Because their two opposite electric charges attract, electrons and protons cling together. Otherwise they would fly off separately into space and we would have no atoms, just a cosmic fog. Instead, we have a structured universe made up of atoms—atoms of helium and hydrogen and the remaining elements. Interestingly, what differentiates helium from hydrogen is that the two electrons in helium each have an opposite "spin"; one is "spin up" and the other is "spin down." Without opposing spins, there would be no helium.

The reality revealed to us by science not only consists of opposites but is also plainly absurd. For example, by causing protons to collide with one another, particles called antielectrons or positrons can be brought into existence. Positrons have been found to be identical to electrons except for one thing: Positrons do not travel forward in time, they travel backwards in time. At the human level, this is like asking us to believe that the days of the week go backwards from Friday to Monday instead of vice versa. Knowing how absurd reality itself is, you should not shrink from putting forward new ideas on the grounds that they are absurd. Perhaps they are good ideas *because* they are absurd.

Opposites and opposite forces not only shape the world but make the world go round. As we all know, the earth is kept in orbit around the sun because the gravitational force that would otherwise pull it into the sun is counterbalanced by the opposing centripetal force that makes the earth want to fly off and away from the sun in a straight line.

The sun itself, of course, and other stars are nothing but huge hydrogen furnaces that would explode outward instantly were it not for the fact that internal gravitation forces pull all the hydrogen molecules inward toward the center. Clearly, physical reality at all levels from the quark to the cosmos is characterized by opposites and by opposing forces either holding things in balance, destroying them, or creating them. Dr. Paul Davies, an English physicist, paints the scene this way:

> There is much competition to be found in nature, between the balance and interplay of different forces, for instance. A star is a battleground of opposing forces. Gravity, which tries to crush the star, struggles against the force of thermal pressure and electromagnetic radiation which try to explode it—forces which in turn are generated by the release of energy due to nuclear interactions. And all across the universe the struggle goes on. However, if the opposing forces were not more or less equally matched, all physical systems would be overwhelmed by one or the other, and activity would soon cease. The universe is complex and interesting precisely because these battles continue over the aeons.[1]

---

1. Paul Davies, *God and the New Physics* (New York: Simon & Schuster, 1983).

## OPPOSITES AT WORK

Nature is lawful. Even its laws can act in contradictory ways. For example, one of its laws is that of cause and effect. The same cause can sometimes produce one effect and at other times, an opposite effect. Water makes the grass grow green, true. But too much water kills the lawn. Braking stops the car, but braking on ice makes the car slide faster. We might call it "the law of opposite effects." The old saying put it well, "The same heat that melts the butter hardens the egg." What is even stranger is that sometimes the effect produces the cause and not vice versa, known as reverse causality. To illustrate, the furnace heats the house and causes the thermometer to rise. When it rises to a certain level—when it has produced the required effect—it triggers an off message to the furnace, causing it to stop. In other words, the very temperature that was to be the effect is now the cause.

Opposites not only work together to create reality, they also dictate that reality can never do anything but change. Change started when a big bang some 15 billion years ago kick-started the universe into being, expelling vast particles of matter and energy outward at an indescribable speed. Built into that explosion were forces of cause and effect, chance and probability, gravity, and magnetism that governed the behavior of those flying pieces. Such is the nature of these laws that they always do two contrary things at the same time—that is, they both create and destroy. Creativity and destruction sprang into intertwined existence the instant time began.

Great minds in science often believe that everything has an opposite even when the opposite has never been seen. The physicist Wilhelm Ritter, who discovered ultraviolet radiation at the age of twenty-five, is one such example. In an article in *The Sciences* in 1993, Sidney Perkowitz remarked about Ritter that he "had strong ideas about unity and polarity as principles of nature, exemplified in the linked but opposing north and south poles of magnetism." Ritter reasoned, said Perkowitz, that since there are infrared rays that lie beyond red in the spectrum of sunlight, they should have polar twins that lie beyond the opposite, violet, end of the spectrum, even though no one had ever detected them or even assumed that they existed. Ritter was right. It was eventually proved that these polar twins exist. They are what we now know of as ultraviolet rays.

Scientists and engineers work with the forces and dynamics of mass, matter, and energy manipulated in the contexts of space and time; indeed, they often do their work with the purpose of shortening or lengthening time or of spatially altering the shapes of material objects. To take a simple example, engineers design machines that require metal to be shaped into blocks or balls or cylinders in order for the machine to be built and operate, and their minds immediately go to work visualizing straight lines, curves, and angles. When we look closely at what they're doing, we know to expect that they are playing games with opposites and paradox.

For example, we generally take a straight line and a curve to be opposites. Yet we can see, with a little thought, that a curve is nothing more than an infinite number of infinitely small straight lines angling away in succession from one another. It is out of this succession of straight lines that a curve appears. Again, we normally think of a circle and a square as opposites. But it is not hard to prove that they are the same thing, namely polygons. How so? If you keep adding sides to a square it turns into a hexagon, an octagon, and so on. The more sides your polygon acquires, the more it comes to resemble a circle. The two opposite things, the circle and the square, deep down are the same thing.

Once again, spheres and cubes are antithetical shapes. If we join a sphere and a cube, we do not get a spherical cube or a cubical sphere but a cylinder. The cylinder is a Hegelian synthesis, a remarkable object that is both straight and curved at the same time and wholly different from either a sphere or a cube. The properties and functional attributes of cylinders are unique, and the world is full of cylindrical objects ranging from the cylinders we use in engines to our cylindrical poles, peppermills, pencils, and pens.

When it comes to paradoxical shapes, the most contradictory and paradoxical of them all is the Mobius strip. The inside and the outside surfaces are one and the same surfaces. Mobius strips are used to record sounds on both sides, and Mobius strip tape recorders run the tape twice as long. Mobius strip conveyor belts and abrasive belts wear equally on both sides. Here is what a Mobius strip looks like:

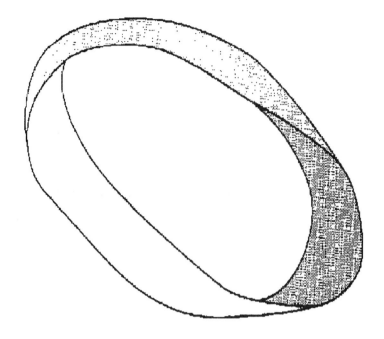

The following limerick captures its weirdly paradoxical character.

> *A mathematician confided*
> *That a Mobius strip is one-sided.*
> *You'll get quite a laugh*
> *If you cut it in half,*
> *For it stays in one piece when divided.*

Every particle has its opposite. For every force in the universe, there is an opposite force. Modern physics proves conclusively that nothing could exist were it not for opposites. Not a particle of matter! Not a bit of energy! Not a single atom or molecule! Not a star or a galaxy, and certainly not an animal or a human being. Moreover, nothing could happen except for forces in opposition to one another. This is not something to be read about and walked away from.

How does all this translate to the workplace? We are all creatures of love and hate, reason and superstition, discipline and license, hope and fear, competition and cooperation. How do all these opposing attributes and impulses cause us to behave? Think about the kind of organizations produced when opposite types of people are put together, such as introverts and extroverts, actives and passives, dominants and submissives. What can we expect to find going on in organizations constructed as they are from people who are composed of opposites, of often conflicting forces and traits?

What can the laws of opposites and paradox tell us about the best way to manage our businesses—systems where people perform such opposite functions as buying and selling, hiring and firing, spending and saving, producing and consuming?

These are questions that people in various occupations are beginning to ask, and they are coming up with fascinating answers. The theoretical and practical study of opposites is an expanding frontier.

But as we study opposites and how they operate, we see that opposites are not only a source of innovation but are also the force behind all change, including destructive change. Change can come about as a result of purely destructive forces, such as earthquakes, epidemics, crimes, and wars. Destruction is the process by which things are taken apart, under the pressure and strain of conflicting forces. It is natural for people to resist destructive changes except when they are in exchange for something better. Such resistance to change is a reflection of character, spirit, and will.

On the other hand, it is easy to love creativity. Creativity is the process of construction, of putting things together to form meaningful new patterns and arrangements. Unfortunately, even creativity can be destructive. To construct, you often must first destroy. To create houses, you cut trees down. To reinvent and re-create organizations, existing positions have to be dissolved, almost always resulting in pain and suffering. The human resources director of a Black and Decker plant that was closed told me of numerous long-term employees weeping during the plant's last day, as some jobs were terminated and others moved to another town.

Once a change occurs, no matter whether destructive or constructive, it spawns problems and opens up opportunities at the same time. Even problems produced by change are opportunities for creative people to do something imaginative. Necessity does become the mother of invention.

## THE PROMISE OF THE PARADOX PROCESS

- In automobiles, we had windshields to see the road ahead, and then innovated with rearview mirrors to see the road behind.
- We normally walk on aboveground sidewalks, but have found it useful to innovate with underpasses or overpasses to cross at busy intersections.
- We normally live in houses built above ground, but with energy prices rising, some people have found it economical to innovate with underground houses.
- Normally our streets and shops are above ground, but in cold winter cities like Toronto or Montreal, we have innovated by building miles of streets and shops underground.
- Private planes got to be bigger and more luxurious to the point where the fun had gone, so we innovated in the opposite direction and designed sparse ultralites that let us fly at speeds of twenty to forty miles an hour with the wind in our faces.
- At one time we assumed that homes, workshops, and offices had to be in fixed locations, but now mobile versions of each are making their appearance.
- At one time we assumed that to be enjoyable salads were and should be cold—until we discovered by experiment and design that hot salads could be equally, and at times more, delicious.
- We had always assumed that hot dogs should be short and stubby—until someone invented the foot-long hot dog to cater to those with bigger appetites.
- Hot dogs had always been bland until someone made them spicy. (Hot dogs with cold drinks have long been a staple hot-cold combo in the American diet. Will future stadium vendors, trained in advertising psychology, sell us cold hot dogs and warm pop and proclaim it a breakthrough idea?)
- We once had to have most things done for us. Now do-it-yourself is a booming field, full of innovations. We have self-study, self-employment, self-service gas stations, and do-it-yourself kits for everything from carpentry to tax preparation and business incorporation. We perform medical tests and diagnoses on ourselves and manage our own savings and retirement plans.
- Traditionally, employees worked for managers, but increas-

ingly the opposite is the case. Managers are now sometimes employed by worker-owners of their own enterprises, as at United Airlines. And each manager is also an employee-owner of the firm.

Reflect on how huge are the dollar implications of each of the above innovations. Think about how they are meeting the needs of today's industrialized, urban world. See how each came about as a result of someone's thinking of opposites to solve a problem and open up opportunities. But most important, notice that many of the ideas could have come to anyone bold enough or unconventional enough to entertain the idea of playing with an opposite and pushing hard enough to make a breakthrough. We can all be such people.

Note also that some of the above inventions and innovations came as the result of doing something that was simply the opposite of what is commonly done—a contrarian mode of thought. Others reflect a two-sided Janusian approach and entail the simultaneous presence of both opposites in juxtaposition. Some are Hegelian in nature and represent a synthesis of two opposites.

Here are some more examples of paradoxical innovations. Reflect on whether they are contrarian, Janusian, or Hegelian, but don't worry if the distinctions sometimes blur.

- The household hammer contains a head for hammering nails in and a claw for pulling them out.
- The common lead pencil with its eraser tip is designed both for putting words on paper and for taking them off.
- Shutters let air in and keep light out.
- Nuts and bolts work because each is threaded in an opposite direction from the other.
- Penknives were designed so that they can both cut and not cut by being opened or closed.
- Reversible belts, sweaters, and the like are great for travel because they provide more outfits from fewer clothes.
- Electronic detectors on parolees' ankles enable them to be free and imprisoned at the same time.
- Prescription eyeglasses can be dark when outside in the sun but light when indoors, so that they are both glasses and sunglasses.

# DEVELOP AN AWARENESS OF OPPOSITES

The most important step in working with opposites is to develop an awareness of them and bring them to the forefront of your mind. Most of us are simply not sufficiently aware of the sheer prevalence and importance of opposites.

When we say one thing is the opposite of another, we mean only that they are opposite in one or more particular attributes or dimensions. Men and women, for example, are not opposites except in the geometry of their sexual equipment—a fact that explains why reference is made to "the two opposite sexes" rather than to two opposite species. Dogs and cats are opposites in a number of ways, but certainly not all. They are opposite, for example, in the fact that dogs think they need to please people but cats think people need to please them. Mansions are the opposite of shacks in size, cost, and comfort, but they are the same in the sense of having roofs, doorways, floors, windows, and ceilings. Thus, what we are always looking for are those elements or aspects in which two things are opposites.

Make some lists of opposites to remind you of their presence and tip your mind off to creative possibilities. You could extend any of the following lists of opposites to encyclopedic length, but right now just make them long enough to raise your consciousness.

The following lists of opposites are grouped by type. Read each list and add three more items to each list.

1. *Physical Opposites*
   Up/down, in/out, left/right, back/front, big/small, beginning/end, thick/thin, north/south, east/west, slow/fast, hard/soft, hot/cold, steam/ice, dark/light, explode/implode, expand/contract, rise/fall, past/future, particle/antiparticle, electron/positron, quark/galaxy.

   1. _____
   2. _____
   3. _____

**2.** *Biological Opposites*
Male/female, young/old, sick/healthy, birth/death, preda-tor/prey, ant/dinosaur, bird/fish, mouse/lion, tortoise/hare, head/feet, left hand/right hand, penis/vagina, mouth/rec-tum, eat/excrete, fight/flight, dominant/submissive.

1. _____
2. _____
3. _____


**3.** *Business Opposites*
Buy/sell, save/spend, profit/loss, revenues/expenditures, hire/fire, own/rent, upsize/downsize, expanding/contracting, ac-quire/divest, president/janitor, purchasing/sales, high tech/low tech.

1. _____
2. _____
3. _____


**4.** *Management Opposites*
Backward-looking/forward-looking; inward-looking/outward-looking; bureaucratic/entrepreneurial; fat/lean; top-down/bottom-up; rule-driven/creative; rigid/flexible; fast/slow, dicta-torial/participatory; amateur/professional, tyrannical/humane.

1. _____
2. _____
3. _____


**5.** *Human Opposites*
Remember/forget, love/hate, forgive/condemn, life/death,

hope/despair, anticipate/recall, forget/remember, memory/imagination, active/passive, energetic/lazy, introvert/extrovert, cold/warm, gullible/skeptical, conscious/unconscious, cops/robbers, giant/dwarf, genius/dunce, hero/coward, saint/sinner, prisoner/guard, nun/prostitute.

1. _____
2. _____
3. _____

**6.** *Social, Economic, and Political Opposites*
Science/superstition, war/peace, wealth/poverty, progress/decline, theistic/atheistic, global/local, barbarian/civilized, elitism/egalitarianism, democracy/dictatorship, liberal/conservative, cooperation/competition, socialism/capitalism.

1. _____
2. _____
3. _____

## WORKING WITH OPPOSITES

Opposites sometimes have certain features we should be conscious of, and they can be of different types. Where each of the pair is completely separate from the other, as with up and down, in or out, dead or alive, left hand and right hand, or floor and ceiling, they are *pure opposites.*

Where each opposite gradually shades into the other, as do night and day, rich and poor, white or black, they are *opposites of continuity.* No two things could be more opposite then are black and white. Yet as you move along the scale from white to black, the white gets less white and slowly turns grayish, then light gray, then gray, then dark gray, then definitely black. With opposites of continuity, at the extremes, at the poles, a difference in degree turns out, in some odd way, to produce a difference in kind. We encounter a

phenomenon that is exceedingly strange and defies logical understanding. That transitional change has been referred to as Engels'
Law, in honor of the German philosopher Friedrich Engels, who
made much of it. Engels' law states, "At a certain point, a difference
in quantity becomes a difference in quality."

That is, at a certain point along the physiographic continuum,
we no longer have hills but mountains. At a certain point along the
continuum of human size we encounter midgets or giants. At a certain point along the pictorial continuum, the pictures are porno-
graphic rather than erotic. At a certain point along the artistic or IQ
continuum, we encounter the genius. At a certain point along the
political continuum, an elected official changes from determined
servant to dictatorial despot.

That polar extremes are different from what lies between them
opens the door to all kinds of creative possibilities. For example,
black and white are put together in the game of checkers, the newspaper photo constructed of black dots on a white background, and
the black/white combination of the traditional tuxedo. Attempts have
been made to create black/white combinations that are more holistic.
The picture below is an oddball example: a white barrel seemingly
emerging from nowhere. In working with opposites, keep in mind
that some opposites are radically different from each other, but only
in degree and amount, like heavy/light or rich/poor.

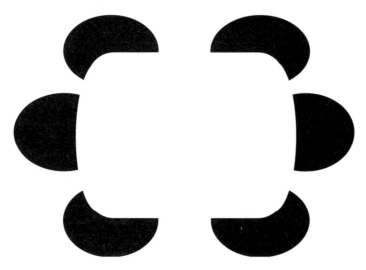

Another example of polarization is big/small. There is big/small polarization in people, houses, and cars. It is amazing how far you can go entrepreneurially by paying attention to even such simple polarizations as big and small. People, for example, come in midget and giant sizes. Midgets and giants are clear-cut opposites, yet the difference is one of degree. But if you stand them side by side, they seem different in kind and not only degree—a midget is a midget and a giant is a giant—no mistaking the two. Every person occupies a height along the spectrum that goes from short to tall, so we talk about tall, short, and average. It's the same with thin and fat. When differences in degree produce differences in kind at either pole, there is an opportunity for entrepreneurship.

Yet another example of polar opposites is the rich and the poor. Again, this is a difference in degree that leads to a difference in kind, and to two opposite kinds of people whose lives and attitudes can be so different that they might as well be from two different planets. The novelist F. Scott Fitzgerald, who liked to write about the rich, said, "The very rich are different from you and me."

## Entrepreneurial Niches

Entrepreneurs and innovators have found market niches in the clothing industry with specialty stores that cater to people who are large in height or weight or both. Some shoe manufacturers do a brisk mail order business targeting people with unusually broad or long feet, and short people who want elevator shoes to make themselves an inch taller. Why not a few large-size seats at special prices on transpacific flights, where comfort is a big factor?

I never realized that the oven in our stove was big until my wife bought our first toaster oven and hung it under the cupboard shelves near the refrigerator. I quickly discovered what a useful gadget this miniature marvel was. I assumed, of course, that it could make toast, and it did. But I eventually discovered that it could roast hot dogs, fry bacon, bake rolls—in short, do almost everything a big oven does, only on a smaller scale. It was nothing but a small version of the oven in our stove. I was also amazed at its low cost; no wonder it was one of the best-selling items to have come out in a long time. Yet this innovation had resulted from someone's simply thinking that an oven could be made smaller rather than larger.

The innovator's mind may wander over existing examples, to come up with new ideas. What's another big/small opposite? A very small freezer or refrigerator? Too late, they exist. Why not stop for a minute and come up with three new product ideas based on something that is the opposite of what is now on the market?

1. _____

2. _____

3. _____

How about joining the opposites to form one new product? Such a device is on the market, manufactured by Comtrad Industries in Midlothian, Virginia. The company makes a portable heater-refrigerator, its use depending on your intentions.

The polarity between rich and poor creates challenges, problems, and opportunities for entrepreneurs and innovators. Examples of poverty-inspired innovations are food stamps, tax exemptions, soup kitchens, hostels, welfare payments, education subsidies, student loans, workfare, and inner-city enterprise zones. Some of these reflect contrarian thinking, in the sense that they involve giving instead of taking from people; others are Janusian, as in the case of student loans that are money first given, then taken back; and others are Hegelian inventions to transform dependent poor people into independent entrepreneurs. Why not come up with one contrarian, one two-sided, and one Hegelian innovation that could help the poor?

1. A contrarian solution:_____

2. A Janusian solution: _____

3. A Hegelian solution:_____

The rich have received more entrepreneurial attention than the poor, since they have so much money to spend. Indeed, there is no end to the creativity lavished on the rich: exotic cruises, safaris, polar expeditions, Everest adventures, jewels, furs, Ferraris, jets, investment funds, charity balls, named museums, and university faculties and chairs. Some innovations are contrarian, as when the rich forfeit comfort and impose physical hardships on themselves, or play at giving money away instead of taking it in. Others are two-sided, earnest attempts to make the poor or middle-class richer, as were those initiatives Henry Ford made.

## Attraction, Repulsion, and Oscillation

Certain opposites attract each other, as do the opposite poles of a magnet. Others are mutually contradictory or antagonistic, such as breaking and joining, boiling and freezing, helping and harming, or cooperating and competing. Yet these contradictory opposites are sometimes found together, even close together. The relationships can be strained, unstable, and unpredictable, but often are productive.

The introverted inventor partners with an extroverted marketer; they have a hard time understanding each other, but they profit mutually from the relationship. The tough superior demands that his subordinates take on heavy burdens of responsibility, then gives them bonuses for doing so; the followers grow in capability, perhaps to the point of competing for their boss's job. Two spouses or business partners have a love-hate relationship; they swing *back and forth* between love and hate, and have interludes where the two attitudes exist at the same time.

Take cooperation and competition. They are often mutually incompatible states, or seem to be. At one time the idea of cooperating with a competitor (except in the illegal form of price-fixing) never entered anyone's mind because it seemed to be contrary to common sense. But strategic alliances, one of the greatest innovations of recent times, are everywhere.

At one time, it was automatically assumed that teams, like committees, would produce a bureaucratic form of group think. It was once believed that individualism and teamwork were as incompatible as oil and water, and that having anything done by a team was a surefire way to douse the flames of creativity, performance, and enterprise. It's now recognized that individual stars can help a business team perform better, while a good team can bring out the best in its individual stars.

## WHO'S BEEN THINKING ABOUT OPPOSITES?

The phenomenon of opposites, their coexistence and mutual dependence, was studied by some of the early Greek philosophers, most notably Anaximander, who lived between 610 and 545 B.C. Anaximander is regarded as the world's first philosopher and the first person in history to examine the world in a rational and analytical manner, trying to figure out how it was constructed. One of his first conclusions about the world was that it was constructed of opposites, like earth and sky and warm and cold, and that there was a dynamic interaction and interdependence among the opposites that he saw. Later, Heraclitus, who lived around 480 B.C., preached that anyone who did not recognize this phenomenon of opposites and their interconnectedness was simply out of touch with reality and had a false view of the world. Only by understanding opposites and their interplay could one make any sense of how the world worked because the world, beneath its apparent chaos and disorder, had a hidden logic driven by opposites. Conflict between opposites produced change. Changes in one direction automatically set off counterchange in the opposite direction, thus producing a new balance, but a balance that was unstable and led to still further changes. This accounted for the paradoxical fact, he explained, that things were always changing and hence the only thing permanent was change itself.

Some of these early scientists went even further and saw change—and the conflict between opposites—as an underlying creative force in the universe that caused the world and everything in it to come into existence. In Western society, the consciousness of opposites and paradox, and their intellectual and practical importance, has ebbed and flowed.

A consciousness of opposites permeated the literary as well as the scientific world of ancient Greece. For example, in his *Poetics,* Aristotle remarked about the play *Oedipus Rex* by Sophocles that "reversal of the situation is a change by which conditions in the play are transformed into their opposite. . . . Thus in the *Oedipus,* the messenger comes to cheer Oedipus and free him from his alarms about his mother, but by revealing who Oedipus really is produces the opposite effect."

In the fourteenth century, Nicholas of Cusa was expatiating on the importance and significance of opposites, describing paradox as *coincidentia oppositorum*—coincidence of opposites—and explaining it as a meeting of opposites or a coincidence of contrasting ideas. His idea that there could legitimately be contrasting ideas on a subject did not sit well with the authorities. And today, particularly during the last five to ten years, there has been a renaissance of interest in the concept of opposites and paradox, in both Europe and North America. This renaissance is reflected in political, economic, and management books on the subject and an increasing flow of articles in periodicals; for example, *Global Paradox* by John Naisbitt, *The Age of Paradox* by Charles Handy, and *The Paradox of Success* by John R. O'Neil.

A spreading interest in paradox is also reflected in the invention and application of new psychotherapeutic techniques; for example, *Making Things Better by Making Them Worse*, by Allen Fay, M.D. This popular book is written in a humorous vein, but there is no dearth of serious works on paradoxical methods for the treatment of mental, emotional, and personality disorders.

A sensitivity to opposites and paradoxes has also been part of Eastern thought for thousands of years, and remains a basic part of everyday thinking. Eastern thought regards opposites as both omnipresent and intrinsically complementary, embodied in the concept of *yin* and *yang,* literally meaning the dark side and the sunny side of a hill. First mentioned in Chinese writings in the 4th century B.C., *yin* and *yang* are generalized to represent the idea that everything comes in opposites, and opposites are to be found in everything that exists, ideally in a harmonious and dynamic balance.

The *yin* and *yang* symbol, shown by the circle on the next page, explains how opposites nestle intimately in perfect companionship, symmetry, and harmony. The circle represents the world, which is composed of opposites. *Yin* and *yang* are opposite in color, but the black part contains a spot of white and the white part contains a spot of black. With the passage of time, the white spot becomes larger, until it occupies all the space that had been black, leaving only a small spot of black. The same process happens simultaneously in the other part of the circle, in the opposite way. When the process of change is completed, everything will have returned to its original state, except black and white will have changed places. The process is ready to start again, and will continue through eternity. The world is both changing and not changing; opposites complement each other, and each opposite contains the seed of the other.

This Eastern view of opposites and change has traditionally been benign and harmonious, whereas Western thought has often expressed admiration for the antagonistic and harsher aspects of change. Perhaps it is time to accord both their truths, and strive for a Hegelian synthesis. Our contemporary view of reality, aided by the discoveries of modern physics, and shared by scientists in both Eastern and Western societies, sees reality and the world process at all levels, from the subatomic to the biological and cosmic, as characterized by simultaneous order and disorder, randomness and lawfulness, creation and destruction, violence and harmony, and permanence and change.

## What to Conclude?

Opposites, opposites, opposites everywhere. Not only atoms and galaxies, but every single thing that exists consists of opposites and opposite forces. When opposite forces are in balance and harmony and nothing is altered, the thing or entity survives. When the balance or harmony of the opposites breaks under internal or external stress, the entity deconstructs into fragments. Then, they either drift apart or join with other fragments from elsewhere to form new wholes, often original in character and with unanticipated properties. This breaking apart and the subsequent joining and forming are what constitute change and creativity. Out of disorder, ineluctably, emerges order. Out of chaos comes the universe. Out of darkness comes light. The inbuilt flux of destruction, creation, and change appears not to have any end that is certain or discernible.

The miracle of creativity, change, and evolution that produced the universe and matter itself had outdone itself when it created life in all its forms, including man. Our successor species will be more conscious, more aware, and more creative; in the meantime, here we are. We are designed with capabilities that allow us to survive and thrive in the midst of change. We have been endowed with the ability to bring constructive change into existence in two ways: either by deliberately creating something new or by altering whatever already is. We have the ability to look at the universe that created us and to contemplate its nature. We have the ability to look at ourselves and to contemplate our own nature. We have been created to be creative and to share in the process of progress and evolution.

Since everything is fabricated in opposites, our answer to the creativity challenge is to find solutions that are contrarian, Janusian, and Hegelian. The Paradox Process, involving the use of opposites, is a tool to help in a task that we are designed by nature to do.

# Chapter 5

# THE PARADOX MIND-SET

"The reasonable man adapts himself to the world. The unreasonable man persists in trying to adapt the world to himself. Therefore, all progress depends on the unreasonable man."

—George Bernard Shaw

Once you see that paradoxical thinking can provide powerful channels along which your creative thinking and action can flow, how do you take advantage of your new insight? That's what the Paradox Process is all about. Paradoxical thought will open the doors to new possibilities and fresh formulations. But the process is no tea party; it calls on all your resources of will, passion, and character. Your whole being will be put to work.

The biggest mistake you could make is to believe that paradoxical thinking is no more than a technical procedure. We live in a techniques, procedures, and methods–based business culture. These techniques and procedures have their place, but so have human will, imagination, and ingenuity. In the Paradox Process you will find a discipline that requires a certain state of mind. I refer to this state of mind as the Paradox Mind-Set.

Some innovative people are in this mind-set so much of the time that it appears to be their permanent state, but this is not so. Much of the time they are happily enmeshed in conventional, mechanical thinking. When they are in a mood to produce new ideas and innovations, however, the mind-set gets turned on and stays on until the task is ended.

Let's look in succession at the seven elements of this critical mood and mind-set. For convenience, I'll phrase them as seven injunctions.

## BE PURPOSEFUL

To be creative takes an overwhelming sense of purpose and mission. When we are creative we attempt to break through, around, and over well-entrenched obstacles of tradition, custom, and belief. Breakthrough solutions and paradoxical innovations thus take energy, determination, and tenacity. Some strong motivational forces will obviously have to go to work.

Where could such strong motivation come from? Only from a desire powerful enough to turn on your whole being. Desire is everything. A powerful desire will arouse intense feeling and cause you to think hard about ways to satisfy it. It will provide emotional energy.

Desire and emotion also need a goal, an objective to focus on, a target whose attainment will satisfy that desire. Purposefulness characterizes everything that lives, whether it is a bee carrying nectar to its hive, a rabbit fleeing from a hawk, or a group of engineers building a new plant. Only highly motivated and purposeful people are likely to put forth the mental and emotional energy that paradoxical thinking takes. Even when discoveries or inventions arise by accident, they always happen to someone who is energetically pursuing some goal. To illustrate: When a mold accidentally landed on a petrie dish and killed a staphylococcus culture growing there, Sir Alexander Fleming, who had long been on the hunt for antibacterial substances, saw that chance had presented him with a gift of enormous importance—penicillin.

How do goals and objectives take form and shape? Goals and objectives begin as visions in our imagination as we look for ways of satisfying our desires. They are pictures in our mind. One might begin with a vision of being independent and owning one's own company but without any idea of what kind of company that might be. Then the vision might crystallize into the definitive goal of owning some kind of software firm. With still more thinking, that goal might narrow down to the specific objective of starting a software firm dedicated to designing and selling human resources management software to government agencies. The goal could proceed from that to be up and going within three months.

*Motivation* and *objective* are very nearly synonymous terms. To be motivated means to have an objective. To have an objective means to be motivated. Purposeful motivation can accomplish remarkable things. Never underestimate the extent to which you can make things happen because you want them to happen. Have the faith and conviction that those things indeed will happen. And never underestimate the power of your unconscious mind to come up with answers.

Objectives can be as plain or as majestic as you want to make them, as long as they serve your visions. Think now of some innovative objectives, some new and different goals that you would like to achieve in your work, and which would be in line with your dreams or visions. Then keep these objectives in mind for later reference, when you take further steps in the Paradox Process.

It is important that you do this exercise and not skip over it because having innovative objectives in mind and being purposeful is an absolute necessity. And they have to be objectives that you are concerned about. There are people who are not goal oriented and purposeful, but they are not people who make breakthroughs and create, invent, or produce innovations.

Write down the three objectives you would like to aim for:

1. _____

2. _____

3. _____

## BE OPEN

The paradox mind-set is one of openness and curiosity. Making creative breakthroughs and inventing new ideas require openness to the world around us, and to some of the vagrant ideas that sometimes float through our minds, often seemingly from nowhere. We also have to open our minds to new information, let new ideas flow in from outside. We have to do more looking and listening. And the openness has to be active. We want to move about, explore, look around, observe, be curious. We want particularly to become attentive to things that we have been ignoring, cultivate the habit of looking at things with a curious eye, and visualize how they could be different from what they are—how they could, indeed, be changed into their exact opposites.

One hitch to openness is that it takes time to explore, muse, reflect, and expose ourselves to new perceptions of reality. Managers often complain that they don't have enough time. But it raises the question: Enough time for what? For doing more of what they are already doing? It turns out not. An American Management Association research study found that two things almost all managers say they want to spend more time doing is thinking and idea generation. But thinking that has any depth, and creative ideas that have any real value, not only takes time but has to be done at those times when we're not being run off our feet.

The bottom line is that to be as open, effective, insightful, and innovative as you ought to be, you must find the time to think, observe, and reflect. There are countless ways in which you can do that. Other people in the same job as yours do it. Time management literature and time management courses can be extraordinarily helpful.

For now, let's recognize that openness and curiosity are at the front end of the paradox mind-set, part and parcel of being purposeful and goal oriented. Take a minute now to look around the room you are in. Look at eight to ten objects in it, one at a time. Then pick three of them and visualize each of their opposites. For example, you see a desk. Visualize your office with no desk. You see a rug on the floor. Visualize it on the ceiling. You see lights in the ceiling. Visualize them on the floor. Now pick three other objects. The exercise may cause you to feel a bit foolish and impractical; that's normal. What will be harder to take will be when other people, including your best friends, tell you your thoughts and ideas are foolish and impractical, or at best eccentric. Remind yourself that people who are relentlessly sensible are not creative. Knowing this, one vice president urges his direct reports to be outrageous in their thinking.

Object 1: _____  The opposite: _____

Object 2: _____  The opposite: _____

Object 3: _____  The opposite: _____

What did you accomplish with this exercise? You forced your-self to experience what it feels like to explore, examine, and turn things around in different and opposite ways.

Now let your mind turn to your company. What are three of your most important products or services? What functions do they perform for the customer? What would be three opposite products or services—that is to say, products or services that perform func-tions that are the opposite of those performed by your present prod-ucts or services?

Here's an illustration of what I mean. If you're in computers, op-posite products could be computer games for learning how to han-dle medical emergencies versus computer games designed just to have fun. Or instead of computer games for the seeing, computer games for the blind. Or instead of fun stuff, how about the opposite, some serious stuff—tax accounting software, software for factory maintenance management, or self-test medical software?

1. Current product
   or service:_____ The opposite:_____

2. Current product
   or service:_____ The opposite:_____

3. Current product
   or service:_____ The opposite:_____

## BE SKEPTICAL

To think paradoxically, you have to be in a skeptical mood. The more skeptical, the better. Paradoxical thinkers don't take it for granted that what is customarily done is the right thing, the best thing, or even a good thing. If everyone does the same thing, chances are good that it may be wrong. Even mindless.

Many general practices and customs are mindless. It is human nature to do things for no reason except that everyone else does them: It's called custom or convention. For example, men used to wear fedoras to the office. To be sure, no great harm was done, ex-cept for the waste of billions of dollars on an impractical and unat-tractive type of head gear. Or consider that men are still mandated to wear suits in many offices, where a conservative jacket, tie, and slacks ought to do fine. Perhaps we should write off such odd and mindless habits as custom, convention, or fashion and let it go at that. It has the great merit of not requiring much thought and, more important, of avoiding attention.

But sometimes important issues are at stake. For instance, lawn watering uses 30 percent of municipal water supplies in the eastern states and up to 60 percent in the West. Water is an increasingly scarce resource, and lawn fertilizer runoff pollutes the nation's water with megatons of destructive chemicals. Add the fact that every week citizens spend hours keeping the grass down to a couple of inches in height while the grass itself fights back, hopelessly trying to reach its proper stature of two feet. Lawns are an American institution, but do they have to be?

It may not be mindless for us to do all this watering, fertilizing, and cutting, but it is definitely mindless for us not to question it. Skepticism may get us somewhere. It has already got some people thinking of how to reinvent the space around our houses. Could not forms of groundcover be substituted for a lawn? Could a grass be invented that did not need so much watering, fertilization, or cutting? Could we at least have a grass that didn't grow so fast, or take so much water and so many chemicals?

Researchers at the University of Alberta think they have already come up with a grass that will grow slowly and only to a very short height. In another instance, a California horticulturist, John Greenlee, explores the natural world for substitutes, wondering, "If grasses can be big and floriferous, why can't they also be the opposite: low, self-effacing, and well-behaved?"[1] If more skeptics and reinventors like these Albertans and Californians work long enough, and use the power of paradox in the process, the day is very likely to come when the lawn is no longer quite what it used to be.

Remember the Hans Christian Andersen story about the emperor's new clothes? A small boy, knowing no better than to see and speak the truth, called out, "But the emperor has no clothes." That broke the spell over the populace, which had been persuaded that the emperor was dressed in fine new clothes, and exposed the truth.

Skeptics are breakers of spells. In a world where vested interests

---

1. Wade Graham,, "The Grassman," *The New Yorker* (August 19, 1996), p. 36.

are anxious for us to believe what they want us to believe, it behooves us to be skeptical. What are the popular spells, assumptions, and delusions in today's business world? Try listing three on the lines below.

1. _____

2. _____

3. _____

## BE CONTRARY

The history of progress in science, art, business, technology, religion, and politics is largely a history of the world's nonconformists and dissidents. To a substantial extent, the industrial revolution in England was carried out by a disaffected religious group—the Dissenters, as they were publicly labeled—who refused to accept the doctrines of the Anglican Church. The Dissenters were also publicly referred to as the Nonconformists. Ostracized to a large degree from the rest of English society and its agricultural economy, they had to resort to a life in trade and industry, where their dissenting and nonconforming minds made them natural innovators.

When people are creative and innovative, they tilt toward skepticism and nonconformity. As you direct your will and energy toward creative goals, your skeptical and contrarian attitudes will increase.

Ever since Humphrey Neill coined the term *contrarian,* it has been applied to anyone in any profession whose disposition is to disagree with popular opinion and go in the opposite direction, except when convinced by reason and evidence that conventional opinions make sense. Contrarians are more inclined by instinct to dissent and to refuse to conform than are most other people. Most people prefer to assent and conform.

If you intend to become more skeptical and contrarian, understand how strong the pressures toward conformity and compliance are. Forty years ago, Solomon Asch, an inventive social psychologist, carried out some extraordinary experiments on conformity to show how strong these pressures are. Asch designed some tough experiments to measure what percentage of people were willing to agree with group opinion *even when they knew the group to be absolutely, totally, and clearly wrong.* He had people look at a straight line, called the "standard line," and compare it with three other lines, A, B, and C, only one of which was the same length as the standard line. The picture below shows the kind of comparison that had to be made.

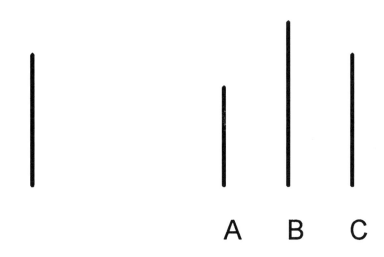

## A    B    C

## Standard Line    Comparison Lines

When a subject entered one of Asch's groups, the subject did not know that the rest of the group were Asch's secret collaborators. The group was primed by Asch to give wrong answers most of the time. The astonishing finding was that only 25 percent of people consistently stood their ground all of the time and refused to go along with the group's wrong opinions.

What can you bring away from the Asch experiment? You can remember that 25 percent hold their ground. You can remember that up to 75 percent of people in your industry, profession, company, or country go along with what they are told by the group, even when it contradicts the evidence of their senses. You can realize that when you innovate you have to stand against popular opinion and do your own thinking. Then when you introduce your innovation you have to anticipate that it will not be judged by whether it is sensible but whether it conforms to what is acceptable. At this point it can take more creative thinking to get the innovation accepted than it did to create it. But that, too, is what creativity and imagination are there for.

Another student of conformity, Harvard psychologist Gordon Allport, described conforming behavior as fitting a J curve in which the overwhelming proportion of people fall into the vertical line of no deviation from the belief or practice in question, and only a very small and diminishing portion flare away at the bottom of the curve. Thinking for oneself is just not a very common habit, except among skeptics and paradoxical thinkers. You need only to look around you to see that conformity and credulity are the norm and that independence and nonconformity are rare.

Yet we were not born that way. We were born contrary as well as compliant. You can see it in the yelling of a small infant only a few days old. The small, angry creature is objecting that something or other is not the way it wants it to be. It has a will and it is demanding. But life gets a lot more complicated, and yelling and screaming won't always work. The infant's life will eventually depend on how well it learns to exercise its will in more complex and subtle ways.

When a baby begins to crawl and grasp, and eventually toddle, it quickly encounters formidable forces of restraint. There are things it is prevented from doing and things it is persuaded to do. Initially, the baby yields to some, accepts some, and balks at others. The battle of wills reaches a crescendo during the "terrible twos."

Eventually the child capitulates, not the parent. Some children become quite accepting, compliant, and yielding, no longer strongly prone to disagree or deviate. But a few others retain an element of contrariness, self-assertion, and/or defiance, usually expressed in some unique way. Such an overtly contrary child stands out and becomes an object of attention or curiosity. It may be described as "difficult."

Do you remember the nursery rhyme?

> *Mary, Mary, quite contrary,*
> *How does your garden grow?*
> *With silver bells and cockle shells,*
> *And pretty maids all in a row?*

Mary will be in for a hard time. Throughout her life she will be under constant pressure to conform, mentally and behaviorally.

The basic truth about the human condition is that conformity is approved of and nonconformity is penalized. It takes determination and consistent effort to maintain an independence of mind. The media, the experts, your industry, your profession, your surroundings never stop trying to suggest what to think. And the pressure is always backed by the assurance that if you think that way, then you are an acceptable, savvy, and admirable person. If you don't agree and conform, then you are difficult, misguided, "not with it." A common conformity-enforcing tactic is to suggest that those who disagree, or who stand up for themselves, are "resisting change." Corporate management of change programs is often directed at getting agreement and obtaining conformity, while at other times it is aimed at encouraging and rewarding the expression of creative dissent and constructive innovation. Which of the two contrary approaches is used depends on the beliefs and value systems of the organization's top leadership.

The process of mental indoctrination thus begins in the crib and continues until you leave this world. Social psychologists call it socialization—the way society controls its members and keeps them in step. On the other hand, the philosopher Immanuel Kant long ago reminded us that we have the moral obligation to take responsibility for our thoughts and opinions. We do not have the right to abdicate this personal responsibility and simply accept the views of institutions and the people who surround us.

Individuals have always been put under pressure to accept things that make no sense.

## Be Paralogical

Creative and innovative thinkers often seem to be illogical, but they aren't. They use logic, but they go beyond it. Their creative mind moves at a level high above simplistic black-and-white, either-or reasoning. They are never limited by existing facts and conventional categories. They are not constrained by the dicta that govern so much of everyday discourse. They move out to the further ranges of human intelligence.

Intelligence takes full wing when it operates with the mind's full battery of cognitive skills. There are eight such skills: (1) memory, (2) logic, (3) reason, (4) judgment, (5) perception, (6) intuition, (7) imagination, and (8) paradox. Every person's brain is equipped with all eight, but whether all eight are utilized is largely a matter of choice and motivation.

The first four are basic cognitive skills, good for everyday conventional living; I call them simply the logical skills. Memory enables us to link what *was* with what *is*. Logic enables us to draw conclusions from facts and principles. Reason allows us to make inferences from known or probable events. Judgment helps us weigh the consequences of our actions. Memory, logic, reason, and judgment are useful and necessary; in many occupations and professions, they do the daily job. The innovator, however, draws on the other four as well, which I call the paralogical skills. *Paralogical* simply means "above logic," and these four paralogical skills—perception, intuition, imagination, and paradox—are the key advanced skills that creativity employs.

Perception enables creative innovators to see things from different viewpoints. Intuition enables them to see and sense the inner meaning of things. Imagination enables them to see what is not there. And paradox enables them to reverse, manipulate, combine, or synthesize opposites. In sum, breakthrough thinkers do not operate only in one cognitive mode but use all the modes together in a fashion that is both logical and beyond logic. When you set out to be purposefully creative, make sure your mind is in a paralogical mood and ready to operate on all eight of its cognitive cylinders.

We have looked at cases where such all-out cognitive work has been successful. The more cases we examine, the more we appreciate the paralogical and paradoxical thinking that created the modern world. It is therefore important to continue to make full use of the processes of perception, intuition, and imagination, giving life to new ideas. This is explored in greater depth in Chapter 8. For now, we need only keep our ears cocked for instances of paradoxical thinking at work. Here's one more example. Contrarian economist E. F. Schumaker expressed a paralogical idea this way:

> All through our lives, we are faced with the task of reconciling opposites which, in logical thought, cannot be rec-

onciled. The typical problems of life are insoluble on the level of being on which we normally find ourselves. How can one reconcile the demands of freedom and discipline in education? Countless mothers and teachers, in fact, do it, but no one can write down a solution. They do it by bringing into the situation a force that belongs to a higher level where opposites are transcended—the power of love.[2]

Paradoxical thinkers point out that often things that are apparently absurd turn out to be true or feasible, that established customs and institutions are sometimes rejected and replaced by their opposite, and that things believed impossible one day turn out to be possible the next. They see reality as semi-surreal. They point to fish that can fly, to countries that change suddenly from communism to free enterprise, to machines that extract heat from ice, to boats made of cement, to criminals who become saints, and to babies conceived in a petri dish.

We need to superimpose intuition, perception, paradox, and imagination on our more prosaic thought processes. The key is to let the imagination go. Don't be afraid of allowing your mind to produce thoughts that initially appear absurd. You never know. Here are three examples of what I mean by absurd thoughts. They happen to be taken from the public sector, but maybe that's where innovation is most needed, anyway.

1. *No more going to school or college.* Everyone learns and studies from early childhood on exclusively through work or play, aided only by interactive exchange with teachers who use television and the Internet. With everyone working, as well as learning, the GNP skyrockets and the deficit vanishes. In addition, the huge social cost of cradle-to-adulthood education almost totally vanishes. School and college buildings are either demolished or put to better use.

2. *No more prisons.* Those found guilty of crimes carry transmitters within their bodies that enable them to be monitored twenty-four hours a day, along with receivers that transmit instructions and

2. E. F. Schumaker, *Small Is Beautiful: A Study of Economics as If People Mattered* (London: Sphere Books, 1973), p. 79.

information to them and chemical immobilizers that can stop them on command from committing more criminal acts. All offenders are required to perform community services for six hours a day, six days a week. They receive a minimum wage and have to support themselves from it. If they take vocational rehabilitation courses three hours a day, they get additional minimum wages for that time.

3. *No more overweight people.* Everyone who is normal weight, neither drinks nor smokes, and can pass a fitness test gets a 20 percent rebate on his or her income tax.

Produce three paralogical ideas of your own:

1. _____
   _____

2. _____
   _____

3. _____
   _____

# BE CREATIVE AND IMAGINATIVE

It isn't enough to be contrary and do the opposite of what is conventional. You also have to visualize, invent, and work out what that opposite thing will be.

It isn't enough to hold two opposites in your mind at the same time. A Janusian solution appears only when you figure out how to juxtapose them to produce something new and valuable. That effort takes insight, creative thinking, and imagination. To take two opposites and conjure up a Hegelian synthesis is an even greater creative achievement.

Let's take a hypothetical example to explore this point. To get ourselves into the proper mind-set, recall that thinking thoughts that are absurd at first glance is an essential part of the game. Now, suppose you decide that on your next vacation you will do something the clear opposite of relaxation and recreation, and a bit absurd seeming. Relaxation and recreation have been your vacation formula for the last fifteen years. What would the opposite be? Work? A *work* vacation may seem a contradiction. Maybe, maybe not.

You begin to visualize some possibilities. One that comes to your mind is three weeks in China, working without pay for a Chinese high school. You would pay your own living expenses and travel there and back at your own cost, all to make it an offer that can't be refused. You would also think up what kind of work you could do that would make the school want you, even for free. It could be quite an adventure if you could pull it off—maybe a lot more enjoyable and stimulating than wandering around Chinese cities on a tour bus, say.

But work in China is only one idea. Perhaps three weeks as a taxi driver in your own city would provide you with some interesting experiences. After all, you muse, why do you have to fall in with the ordinary stereotype of what a vacation should be?

You start to wonder if there could be a Janusian solution to your vacation problem. You muse about how opposites can often be employed together in some complementary, mutually reinforcing form. This work vacation could be combined with fun and play. After all, there are twenty-four hours to the day, and the idea was never to work during all of them. Note that imagination is an inescapable and essential part of paradoxical thinking. Once again, you let your imagination loose.

Use your imagination even more, and take still another step. How about producing a Hegelian synthesis—one where work and play are so closely combined that you can't tell which is which? If you are a first-class golfer, your unpaid work might be acting as a pro's assistant at a Beijing golf club. Then you could spend your time playing golf, coaching rising young Chinese executives to improve their game, and teaching the pro some management techniques for running his shop better. For three weeks you would have transformed recreation into work and work into recreation. So you are not a golfer. Try to think up a work-play synthesis based on your favorite hobby. In any case, use your imagination to come up with a Hegelian solution, just as it did with the contrarian and Janusian solutions.

## Be Courageous

Since opposites are basic to the real world, you'd think that thinking paralogically and paradoxically would be instinctive. But try to actively imagine a poor banker, a compassionate corporate raider, fast molasses, dry water, white licorice, a square wheel, a transparent boulder, a flying turtle, a thin wrestler, a lewd nun, an honest liar, a shy real estate agent, or a kindly sadist. To succeed requires putting pressure on the brain. It may also seem a bit foolish to think such strange thoughts.

People often fear to do anything that looks foolish or strange, even if only to themselves. As Fritz Perls describes it:

> Where people lack imagination it is always because they are afraid even to play with the possibility of something different from the matter-of-fact to which they cling for dear life. The ability to achieve and maintain an interested impartiality between imagined opposites, however absurd one side may seem, is essential for any new creative solution of problems.

Nor has Perls been the only one to recognize that absurdity and creativity are connected. Winston Churchill remarked that "every new idea has an aspect of the absurd when first presented." He added, "No idea is so outlandish that it should not be considered with a searching but at the same time with a steady eye." If we agree with Perls and Churchill, the challenge is to overcome the fear of the absurd, that discomfort created whenever we contemplate something that is the opposite of common practice.

To test ourselves, let's do some more exercises on paradoxical thinking. Try what Perls is speaking of—namely, to put two opposites in your mind and hold them there, even though one seems absurd, and examine them both with impartiality.

As a start, here are a few that come to my mind, and then you can add those that come to yours.

- A gentle bull running from a vicious cow
- A dessert of dill pickles smothered in chocolate sauce

- A poverty-stricken capitalist country that borrows money from a wealthy socialist state
- A born-again Larry Flynt sponsoring a speaking tour by Mother Teresa
- A room with mirrored floors and carpeted ceilings
- Underwater high-rises
- Diets designed for fattening the underweight
- Time management programs for the underemployed
- Empathy training programs for courtroom prosecutors
- Silent skidoos
- Management consultants who claim not to know the answers

Your list:

1. _____
2. _____
3. _____
4. _____
5. _____

In the days of Christopher Columbus, most people "knew" that the earth was flat, even though from the time of the ancient Greeks some educated people had proved that it was round. Sailors "knew" by sailing long enough they would sail over the edge and descend into the abyss of space. As any fool could plainly see, particularly when on the ocean, the earth was certainly flat. Centuries later, "sailors' suspicion syndrome" still exists about any idea that sounds absurd, *even when it can be proved by logic to be sound.* Logic and evidence do not always convince. As the old saying goes, "A man convinced against his will remains of the same opinion still." People often believe what they want to believe rather than what is true.

After Columbus came the most absurd announcement of all: the announcement by Nicolaus Copernicus that the sun did not circle the earth but only appeared to do so. This Polish astronomer cited thousands of astronomical observations to prove that his observation was true and that the common belief was the result of an optical illusion. This was a disturbing idea, this "Copernican paradox," because it undermined the security that came from believing the earth was the center of the universe. The Copernican paradox sits with us today as a collective social memory, a reminder of how wrong people can be.

Earlier in this century, humanity experienced the shocks of relativity theory, then quantum mechanics, then the Big Bang explanation for the creation of the universe. The reality is that the sun is hurtling through the universe at a frightening speed, us with it. Given the fact that paradigm shifts are mentally and emotionally disorienting, and that these shifts are more frequent now than in the past, it is no surprise that existential fear and anxiety is on the rise.

Franklin D. Roosevelt roused the American nation to action during the 1930s by helping it realize "We have nothing to fear but fear itself." Courage is our greatest answer. Philosopher Immanuel Kant spoke of the "decision and courage to be oneself without depending on another's guidance." He urged people to "have the courage to depend on your own understanding!"

Overcoming fear takes courage. Courage is the determination to press ahead and act in spite of fear. In *Love and Will*, psychiatrist Rollo May explained how strong our wills can become when we have a passionate interest in something, a love for it. May devoted another book to the connection between courage and creativity, *The Courage to Create*. It takes courage to create, because creativity means taking chances and exposing oneself to psychological, social, or economic risk. The best tonic for stimulating courage is a goal to which you are passionately committed, a goal strong enough to keep you going despite fear and adversity.

The following exercise should give you some time to reflect on the subject of courage. Read each and write whatever comment comes to mind. Put a score from 1 to 10 at the end of your comment, showing how significant you thought the statement was. There are no correct or incorrect answers.

   **1.** *How over that same door was likewise writ,*
        Be bold, be bold, *and everywhere* Be bold.
        *Another iron door, on which was writ,*
        Be not too bold.
                    —Edmund Spenser (1552–1599)

Comment: _____

_____

**2.** *Stand upright, speak thy Thoughts, declare*
*The truth thou hast, that all may share;*
*Be bold, proclaim it everywhere:*
*They only live who dare.*
               —Lewis Morris (1805–1907)

Comment: _____

_____

**3.** *A decent boldness ever meets with friends.*
               —Homer (700 B.C.)

Comment: _____

_____

**4.** *No one reaches a high position without daring.*
               —Publilius Syrus (42 B.C.)

Comment: _____

_____

**5.** *And what he greatly thought, he nobly dared.*
               —Homer (700 B.C.)

Comment: _____

_____

**6.** *Rest not; life is sweeping by;*
*go and dare before you die.*

*Something mighty and sublime,*
*Leave behind to conquer time.*
                    —Goethe (1749–1832)

Comment: _____

_____


**7.** *He was a bold man that first eat an oyster.*
                    —Jonathan Swift (1667–1745)

Comment: _____

_____


**8.** *The prudent see only the difficulties,*
*The bold only the advantages*
*of a great enterprise; the hero sees both;*
*diminishes the former and makes the latter*
*preponderate, and so conquers.*
                    —Laveter (1741–1801)

Comment: _____

_____


**9.** *You will never do anything in this world without courage. It*
*is the greatest quality of the mind next to honor.*
                    —James L. Allen (1849–1925)

Comment: _____

_____


**10.** *Most men have more courage than even they themselves*
*think they have.*
                    —Fulke Greville, Lord Brooke (1554–1628)

Comment: _____

_____

**11.** *He who loses wealth loses much;*
*he who loses a friend loses more;*
*but he who loses his courage loses all.*
        —Cervantes (1547–1616)

Comment: _____

_____

**12.** *Courage is fear holding on a minute longer.*
        —George S. Patton (1885–1945)

Comment: _____

_____

**13.** *Aspire rather to be a hero than merely appear one.*
        —Baltasar Gracian (1601–1658)

Comment: _____

_____

**14.** *What would life be like if you had no courage to attempt anything?*
        —Vincent van Gogh (1853–1890)

Comment: _____

_____

## CONCLUSION

The Paradox Process is not a mental technique or procedure that can be carried out in a simple straightforward way. Instead it is a process that begins with a passionate and purposeful commitment to deeply felt goals and objectives, and is carried along by the powerful motivation that such commitment supplies. Strong motivation, and the will to think independently, provides the necessary courage to look with a skeptical eye on much that is around you.

Courage generates a will to question, explore, and challenge what most people take for granted. Courage is being contrary minded enough to entertain the possibility that the opposite of what is accepted may be valid. When you visualize something that seems initially absurd, you will resist the temptation to drop the thought. Instead, you will keep thinking it and will remind yourself that thinking such a thought takes courage. And still more courage will be needed to resist the criticism that your new idea will evoke.

Armed with courage, you will be able to keep the two opposites in your mind at the same time and be impartial about evaluating each. You will explore the relationship—how they each may need the other, how each may have its place, how one may turn into the other, and how they might fuse into a synthesis that produces something new. This constitutes the seven-part paradox mind-set.

# Chapter 6

# THE PARADOX PROCESS IN ACTION

"Oil companies expect to drill nine empty wells for every one that flows. Getting it wrong is part of getting it right."

—Charles Handy

Now that we have established the proper mind-set, it is time to get down to the Paradox Process itself, visualized as a series of steps. In this chapter I present case studies to show how the process has yielded breakthrough ideas. No matter what your business, there are some ideas you can find in these examples that, through concept displacement, could be put to work for you. The law of concept displacement says it's quite legal to take an idea from one field and apply it in transmuted form to another field. The main purpose of these examples, however, is to help you gain greater insight into the process and deepen your commitment to paradoxical thinking.

## STEPS IN THE PARADOX PROCESS

The first step, you recall, is to clarify your vision. You already have visions of things you desire or you wish to achieve. It may be a career success, reaching your retirement years, a summer home, a future holiday, or a best-selling management book. Visions are etched in general terms and are always hazy. You also recall that for a vision to become a reality it has to be transformed into goals and objectives.

The steps in the process are as follows:

### Steps in the Paradox Process

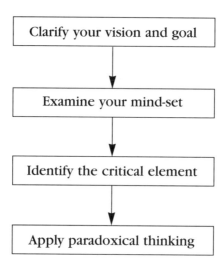

The best way to understand the Paradox Process is to apply it to a hypothetical situation. Suppose the area in front of your house is looking a little seedy. Your vision—your goal—had always been to have everything looking smart. But you've let things go. You decide to use this problem as an opportunity for creating something more attractive than ever before.

You check out your mind-set. Are you prepared to be purposeful, open, contrary, skeptical, paralogical, and creative? You take a strategic approach. Strategy examines a situation in order to focus on the critical elements that need action. You look around to see what the critical elements of the situation are and note that the paint on the two white Adirondack lawn chairs is chipped and peeling. Time to start thinking of opposites and alternative maneuvers.

A simple contrarian opposite of two chairs is no chairs; that option is dismissed—you want the chairs. Another contrarian opposite of two chairs at the front of the house is chairs at the back of the house. No, you want the chairs where they are. Another opposite of peeling and worn paint is clean new paint; that way, they'll be good as they were. But still another contrarian opposite is no paint: The chairs could be stripped down to the natural wood and given a transparent protective coat. No, you don't want that. The opposite of white is black. Paint them black? No, that wouldn't look right.

Now, you mentally try a Janusian route. How about having the boards alternating one black and one white? A chair that's both black and white at the same time. A good idea, but not good for this setting. That would look good at the swimming pool maybe, but not too practical there, anyway.

Finally, you think of taking a Hegelian route: a synthesis of the opposites. How about mixing black paint and white paint? Gray might look good and would blend in nicely with the color of the driveway and the bricks of the house. That's it. Terrific. You go with the gray. You would never have thought of it, except for your new habit of thinking in opposites. Just what you want: a new and more elegant element in the front yard.

Now you look at another critical element in the appearance of the front: that rosebush near the front entrance. Too bad the roses are gone in the winter and will not be back until spring. Instead of roses that go, the opposite—roses that stay—would be a delight. Too bad the cold weather prevents that; the rose is a deciduous shrub. Route 1 suggests the opposite: a bush covered with a mini-greenhouse—say, a transparent glass or plastic sphere—and heated by a single 100-watt lightbulb. Would it look good? Probably not, unless you were in the far north and really desperate for the sight of a few live flowers. Or instead of a mini-greenhouse covering a single bush, how about a large greenhouse covering the whole walk for twenty feet from the house? When you exit the house, you walk through this greenhouse. Too expensive by far, but not a bad idea for those who could afford it. (You recall a luxurious apartment condominium in Montreal, where the temperature is a steady 10 degrees below Fahrenheit, through all of January. The rear of the building has a huge glass-domed tropical garden reaching right up to the topmost apartment. Residents can sit in their shirtsleeves on the balconies in January, enjoying a warm day.)

Back to your problem. How about a contrarian opposite: a rosebush that blooms in winter but not in summer? Or a Janusian solution: a bush that blooms in both summer and winter? Could it be done through gene-splicing? Didn't you read about a new frost-resistant turnip—a Hegelian synthesis—created by infiltrating the turnip with genes from a cold-water fish? A year-round rosebush might not be that impossible. Maybe some research lab is already working on the invention of a winter flowering rose. Is this an entrepreneurial opportunity?

You may dwell on this challenge for days, put the question on the back burner from time to time as you go about doing other things. You look at your problem from different points of view, let your imagination run wild, daydream now and then. An idea may come during the night; you may actually dream about the problem and recall your dream.

## APPLICATIONS OF THE PARADOX PROCESS

### Investment Management

In the world of finance, the idea of thinking in opposites and being contrary is well known. Many investment management experts carry a deep consciousness of contrary thinking as part of their world view. The impact of Humphrey Neill's contrary thinking on the investment world has been incalculable.

There is now a class of portfolio managers known as "contrarians." Larry Kennedy, portfolio manager at Guardian Capital Group Limited, an investment company headquartered in Toronto, is one such contrarian. To Kennedy, the most important things in contrary thinking are its emphasis on the investor's being capable of logical and independent thought and not being concerned about appearing to be different. To be a contrarian, he says, it's sometimes necessary "to love the stocks that people love to hate." He quotes the great economist (and hugely successful investor) John Maynard Keynes, who said, "If everyone is universally agreed about the merits of a particular investment, it's inevitably too dear and therefore unattractive."

Paul Stephens is a U.S. fund manager who lives and breathes the contrarian attitude—to the extent of managing a fund that's called the Contrarian Fund. He tries to buy stocks when they are out of favor or "cheap." You'll see the Contrarian Fund regularly advertised in *Forbes, Fortune*, and other business magazines. But every contrarian has spins over which he or she overlays the contrarian approach. In Stephens' case, it is his visionary interest in the future. One thing Stephens foresees is huge growth in the demand for natural resources, as billions of people in the emerging economies of the world start to demand more consumer goods.[1]

## Banking

The contrarian attitude can color the atmosphere of an entire financial house. The Bank of Nova Scotia, for example, is an international banking complex with over 30,000 employees in countries around the world. Bill Lomax, recently executive vice-president of human resources, singled out contrarian thinking as something deliberately engaged in whenever the bank faced any important question of policy or direction, whether financial or not. The bank has taken the contrarian principle far beyond its original application. Whereas other large Canadian banks concentrated on growing their business primarily inside Canada, the Bank of Nova Scotia emphasized business largely outside of Canada.

Indeed, this bank's frank devotion to contrarian thinking has had effects outside its corporate walls. To illustrate, the bank's top executive team played a major role in the late 1980s by persuading the world's banking community to take a new look at the indebtedness of Third World countries. Specifically, it stressed that these developing countries were potential markets for lender countries. But stubborn insistence on traditional demands for full and prompt payments of outstanding loans could well be against the lending countries' own best interests. The bank's assertive challenge of orthodox banking practice won the day, and the world's banks shifted their position and began negotiating new payment sched-

---

1. *Investor's Business Daily*, 12, no. 204 (January 30, 1996).

ules. As a result, the economic suffering of these third-world companies was reduced and they have grown to become better and better markets for today's bankers.

## Truck Insurance

Graham Goodchild, a financial services executive based in Toronto, is easily classified as a contrarian and an iconoclast, little impressed by orthodox business practices and not hesitant to act on his own convictions. His contrarian attitude often leads him in to paradoxical solutions to problems—breakthrough solutions to problems others had seen as insurmountable.

Goodchild had taken over the job of CEO of a company that supplied insurance to the long-haul trucking industry. The company was doing poorly when he joined it, and it was his job to lead it out of the wilderness. Conventional wisdom was to focus on the top line rather than the bottom line, in the hope that continuous growth would enable the company to get better. But Goodchild believed that industry facts disputed both the wisdom and the common sense of that belief.

It soon became clear to him that to improve the company's profitability, the best strategy would not be to get more customers and more revenues, as it had been up until then. (Normal practice is to increase business in order to support your overhead and add to profits.) Instead, he decided to selectively get rid of the company's bad accounts, knowing full well that the action would result in substantial reductions in revenues.

Like many strategists, he likes to cite Pareto's law: 80 percent of problems come from 20 percent of the customers, the products, the employees, or whatever. So do 80 percent of profits, he adds, but from a different 20 percent. Goodchild set out to unearth the problem accounts.

Fifteen hundred of the largest accounts were examined and evaluated to determine which the company wanted to continue to work with. It took two months to review all the files with all staff involved. Out of $10.5 million in revenues, the company cut $1.5 million by terminating problem accounts. As a result it ended up with a net revenue shortfall of $600,000 but a bottom-line improvement of over $1 million, all within a year. "By reducing revenues,"

Goodchild says, "we improved profits." As only a good paradoxical thinker could, he proved that sometimes less can be more.

## Corporate Organization

*Fortune* magazine calls Dee Hock the "father of the bank card," and with good reason. His was the guiding brain behind the invention of VISA about twenty years ago and he was VISA's first CEO. VISA's annual sales volume has now passed the trillion-dollar mark. Now a universal currency that transcends national boundaries, VISA is accepted by 12 million merchants in more than two hundred countries. In 1995, it was used by 450 million consumers.

VISA employs an unorthodox and radical form of corporate organization founded on paradoxical principles. Indeed, the very key to its success has been a new concept in corporate organization, which Hock refers to as *chaordic*. A chaordic organization combines the two opposing principles of chaos and order in a single Hegelian synthesis. The Internet is an example of what a chaordic organization is and how it operates.

The chaordic concept means that, like the Internet, VISA is designed to grow spontaneously and freely, somewhat like a biological system. Unlike the traditional business organization, which is planned and controlled from a central locus of power, it is self-organizing. Yet all the member banks that are part of the VISA organization adhere to certain principles and rules. Hock describes a *chaord* as "any self-organizing, adaptive, nonlinear, complex organism, organization, or community, the behavior of which harmoniously blends characteristics of both order and chaos."

Another part of the VISA paradox is that the fiercely competing banks that own the right to employ VISA cooperate zealously in protecting VISA's principles and rules. Competition and cooperation sit side by side in Janusian juxtaposition. In terms of our own models of paradox, VISA is therefore both Hegelian and Janusian.

Both VISA and the Internet have grown at a breathtakingly exponential rate—illustrating what happens when the enormous power of local and decentralized initiative and enterprise goes to work to freely pursue a common vision and is bound by a belief in certain basic principles and beliefs.

Dee Hock now heads a nonprofit organization called The Chaordic Alliance. Its function is to help enterprises and institutions organize according to chaordic principles.

## Life Insurance

Some innovations are plain vanilla. This example lacks the glamor of a new product or the drama of a labor-management conflict, but it involved thinking that saved a tidy sum of money for the company concerned. It is amazing how much costly but unnecessary work is done because a practice is followed whose purpose had never been questioned. My friend David Eustace, a writer of novels and a former insurance company CEO, tells me of the contrarian thinking of Murray Marvin, the former president of The Life Insurance Company of Alberta: One day Marvin found himself ruminating on how the accountants spent many hours every month, at a considerable cost, posting the monthly premium payments. Ninety-seven percent of policyholders paid their premiums with unfailing diligence every month. Their payments were duly registered in the books. The 3 percent who did not pay did not get entered, yet they were the ones that needed the attention. So Marvin reversed the bookkeeping practice: He had the accountants stop making entries on payments made. They began to make entries only for the accounts that had not been paid. At first the accountants were disturbed by Marvin's idea because it challenged the conventional wisdom of the accountant's trade, but in no time they were comfortable with this upside-down innovation.

## Philanthropy

Ordinarily the game of finance consists of getting money, not giving it away. For a wealthy financier to give money away would seem to be a contradiction. However, defying conventional definitions, George Soros does both on a gargantuan scale, taking and giving in amounts so lavish as to take your breath away. In the world of finance, he is the ultimate paradox. He is a financier and philanthropist combined in a single person—a finanthropist, you could say.

Soros has built himself an $11 billion financial empire centered on his Quantum Fund, which makes money by the oceanful. On the other hand, his Soros Foundation gives it out in rivers and torrents, at the rate not of millions but hundreds of millions a year. What knits the making and the giving together is a philosophy. In fact, Soros began his career as a philosopher; his money making came later.

As a young graduate student in England, George Soros was deeply influenced by the lectures of Karl Popper. Popper was a post-World War II philosopher who wrote in praise of the open society and against those he called its enemies—enemies who preferred society to be closed and authoritarian. The open society is characterized by freedom, opportunity, creativity, and the unpredictable and undetermined. Soros's Quantum Fund is a metaphor for the Popper philosophy because of its tie-in of nomenclature with the new physics of quantum mechanics, whose central principle is indeterminacy. For Popper, money buys freedom and creativity for people, and freedom and creativity create wealth. The circle is closed.

Soros's breathtaking financial largesse is directed mainly at the emerging free-market economies of eastern Europe, with the goal of helping ensure their survival. The money he pours into some of these countries is so great as to compare in effect with what even the governments of these countries themselves can do. His unorthodox financial strategies and strong views about the social, economic, and moral responsibilities of capitalists have made Soros an exceedingly controversial figure in the field of finance.

## Computers

Peter Norton, who sold his computer software company for $300 million, is a paradoxical thinker. His wealth and success came out of innovations in the computer field. Norton is known to computer users mainly through his famous Norton Utilities, a set of software programs that almost every computer buff in the world has owned. One of Norton's first inventions was a paradoxical utility he called "Unerase," the purpose of which was to recover computer files that had been accidentally erased.

Unintended erasures are a computer user's nightmare. The paradoxical idea of unerasing what had been erased seemed absurd except to someone who understood computers as well as Norton did. He knew it could be done and made it his objective to do it.

Norton's independent spirit and his nonconformity—essential to paradoxical thinking—is reflected in his personal life as well as his business career. For example, Norton spent five years in a Zen Buddhist ashram. Seen on the surface, he has been said to fit the stereotype of a computer nerd to a T. But the reality is that Norton is not only a giant in computer history but a collector of modern art and a well-known patron of rising new artists.

## Computer Peripherals

A risk of failure haunts all new product launches, whether they be as fundamental as food or as exotic as computer peripherals. Conner Peripherals makes hard disk drives for high-speed, high-capacity microcomputers. The company solved the new product failure problem by using an explicitly backward strategy of business: The company will not design and/or manufacture a product until it has first sold it to a big enough customer. The corporate slogan is "Sell-design-build."

There are several advantages to this approach. The necessary millions in R&D funds are guaranteed in advance; also, the design can be evolved step by step in consultation with the purchaser. The latter virtually ensures that the product will be designed to suit the needs of the market. Other purchasers will then be sure to follow.

## Biotechnology

By doing the opposite of what they had been doing, Nicole Provost and her research team at Bothell, Washington's Cellpro, Inc. probably saved the life of their company president. Forty-nine-year-old Rick Murdoch had been diagnosed with lymphatic cancer. After undergoing four months of unsuccessful chemotherapy, Murdoch's one remaining option was a bone-marrow transplant. Unfortunately, the success rate for such transplants was low.

The first step in this procedure is to extract from the patient's bone marrow a collection of what are called stem cells, cells that manufacture blood. But how to rid the collected stem cells of all cancer cells without also destroying the stem cells themselves? Up until that time, no reliable solution had ever been found.

Provost's research team had only six to eight weeks in which to find a solution, no time at all compared to the year in which such a research breakthrough could normally be expected to be made—if indeed it were to be made at all. If it were, Provost told me, this breakthrough would be their boss's "one shot." Otherwise, there would be little hope for his survival.

Although faced with what seemed to be an impossible challenge, the team had no choice but to go all out: They researched the problem around the clock for seven days a week. It helped that the team was armed to the teeth with scientific knowledge, experience in this kind of biotech research, and knowledge of what other researchers had been doing. But most important, they were almost superhumanly motivated by the need to save Murdoch's life.

During one of the team's frequent brainstorming meetings, the breakthrough finally occurred. All alternatives and options had been exhausted except for one: doing the reverse of what they had been doing. Instead of first collecting the stem cells and then purging them of cancer cells, they would try to first purge the cancer and then collect the cells. That turned out to be the solution! The collected cells had no visible cancer cells among them. A year after treatment with radiation, chemotherapy, and the new bone-marrow transplant procedure, Murdoch showed no signs of cancer.

The team's research process included a great deal of trial and error, conscious examination, and testing of all solutions, alternatives, and options—including frequent use of *gedanken* experiments, experiments carried out first in the mind and only later at the bench. As the team proceeded, periodic illuminations occurred, helping them to find their way forward. One of those "clear, defining moments" took place when Provost's team realized that the solution that could save Murdoch's life was not necessarily the same kind of solution that would be needed to produce a marketable product.

Provost also explained that a number of conditions were present to make success possible. One was the intense motivation that caused the team to work and think virtually nonstop. Another was the clarity of the objective and the presence of a well-defined time line. Moreover, every necessary resource was made available without stint or limitation. Finally, the project had top management's complete support. Such a combination of ideal conditions is rare in the life of a research team, Provost pointed out. She told me that all these conditions created a team in which the members were unreservedly supportive of one another, stayed in close communication, and worked harmoniously and energetically hour after hour, day after day.

## *Entertainment*

Torontonian Ed Mirvish and his son, David, own three of the world's most important theaters: the Royal Vic in London, England, plus the Royal Alexandra and the Princess of Wales in Toronto. Ed and David are two reasons why Toronto is the third largest theater center in the English-speaking world, after New York and London.

Ed Mirvish not only is a study in habitual paradoxical thinking, but is a paradox himself. Everyone in Toronto knows and loves him. He has made a fortune from aggressive discount retailing and an advertising style based on outlandish self-promotion and a constant stream of humorous, amiable, and irreverent remarks. In actuality, Mirvish is a modest man, his self-promotion a clever parody on self-promotion. His store—whimsically called Honest Ed's—is visited by 20,000 people a day.

This is a lover of the performing theater, of the best the modern stage has to offer, whose business base in discount retailing is as philistine as they come. Despite his wealth, Ed, at age eighty-one, instead of taking it easy as convention dictates, still comes to his store every morning at 8:00 A.M. to do a full day's work.

When Walmart's came to Toronto in 1994, Ed noticed how the chain had people eagerly greeting customers and offering to help them. In response, he pointed to a large sign in his store that says: "Don't bother our help; they have their own problems." The text under this sign explains that the store tries to keep prices to an absolute minimum, and one way is to offer customers the least possible service in order to have the smallest number of employees. But if you go to one of Honest Ed's restaurants (he owns two), you can expect all the personal service and attention that you don't get at his store.

## Publishing

The United States is famed for flooding the export world with outstanding business books by American writers. But Norman Bodek, founder of Productivity Press in Oregon, created his company by doing quite the opposite: He constructed a business based on importing management knowledge. Bodek imported Japanese management books, translated them into English, and marketed them in the United States. Later, he marketed these English-language translations internationally, often having them translated into other languages.

Perfectly willing to be both conventional and unconventional at the same time, Bodek now also publishes, translates, and exports North American works to foreign countries.

## Manufacturing

Innovators who act in a paradoxical manner are not new to the business world. When Henry Ford decided to raise wages to the unbelievable level of five dollars a day, it was thought absurd because it violated common sense. He was doing the opposite of what business people thought was in their best interests. But when Ford explained that his 200,000 workers were all potential customers for his cars, it made sense to him to pay the highest wages he could afford.

Ford had chosen wages as a critical element in his strategic situation, but looked at those wages in a way opposite to convention. His thinking was paradoxical. He saw a potential wage increase not as a problem but as an opportunity.

One of Ford's dominant traits was skepticism regarding almost all business practices of his day. He had the courage to think for himself, and his action on wages was characteristic of this.

Today it is commonplace, although not universal, to see high wages as a strategy for business success. It is commonplace in high-tech companies that know they can outplay their competitors only by having smarter people, so they use high wages to get those smarter people. And the wages need not be wages in the usual sense, but may be shares in ownership or in profits.

*Design*

John Langdon's name, shown below, reads the same upside down as it does right side up, a feature you can check by turning this book upside down. John is a typography and corporate logo designer who also teaches in the College of Design Arts at Drexel University in Philadelphia. His educational background is English literature, but his way of looking at the world is also extracted from Eastern philosophy and modern physics. This philosophy and science background impels him to see things in terms of opposites, symmetries, and syntheses. His love of words, and a native inclination for art and form, has drawn him to the field of typography.

In particular, Langdon has built a unique professional practice based on designing and marketing ambigrams. An *ambigram* is a word that reads the same upside down as right side up, or the same from right to left as from left to right, or the same when you look at it in a mirror as when you read it on the page. However ingenious the ambigram may be, it must also be aesthetically pleasing. If it is to serve as a corporate logo, it has to capture the spirit of the business that it represents. Here's the ambigram of John's name.

And here's the logo he designed for the rock music group Jefferson Starship. If you hold it in front of a mirror, it still reads the same. That's because the two words, *star* and *ship*, are mirror images of each other.

The logo below was created for a touch dancing club whose interior design was art deco. The logo was designed to be etched on a large piece of glass in the lobby and mounted so that it could be read from both sides.

The following ambigram was designed for Edwards Enterprises, a recycler of paper and plastics. Not only does it read *E* and *E*, but quite appropriately it cycles and recycles.

**Edwards Enterprises, Inc.**
RECYCLERS OF PAPER & PLASTIC

Finally, here is an invertible logo characterized by an unusually neat, simple, perfect symmetry. It's the logo of Suburban Transit Network.

The best way to learn more about ambigrams and their connection with Eastern philosophy and modern physics is to read Langdon's book on the subject, *Wordplay*. Appropriately, its vertically reversible title reads as shown below.

Langdon's foundations in philosophy and science are exemplified in the following ambigram, with its expression of the ambiguous nature of the wave-particle (wavicle) theory of electromagnetic radiation.

His love of words and language is highlighted in another of his ambigrams, this one on the Irish author James Joyce, whose genius at wordplay is unparalleled. The *James* is easy to see, but can you find the *Joyce*?

If you'd like to see more of John Langdon's ambigrams, go into his website at Drexel University: **http://design.coda.drexel.edu/ faculty/johnlangdon/wordplay.html.**

# Chapter 7

# CREATIVE LEADERSHIP IN AN ERA OF CHANGE

"Innovation is our oldest tradition."
—Slogan of John Labatt Limited

The job of leaders is to lead their enterprises out of the past, through the present, and into the future. Anything else they do, no matter how important, must be in support of that function. Furthermore, leaders need to understand that change and innovation have brought the world to where it is today and that these same processes will lead us to our destiny.

Knowing that history is the story of change and innovation, leaders also know that they have to be innovators and agents of change themselves. It is their role to stand astride the flow of change. But many who have called themselves leaders have not been so. They are pseudo-leaders who equate leadership with tradition, status, and authority.

Real leaders have always been practitioners of the Paradox Process, without calling it that. They have been purposeful, open, skeptical, contrary, courageous, paralogical, and creative. They use memory, logic, reason, and judgment, but these qualities are not alone what makes them leaders. They have had primarily to draw on their ability to perceive, intuit, imagine, and think paradoxically—otherwise they could not have been the persons they were nor accomplished what they did.

## WHAT LEADERS SAY

While pseudo-leaders may be indifferent or resistant to change and innovation, real leaders most certainly are not. Instead, they are passionate believers in creativity and are committed to it wholeheartedly. From science to business, and manufacturing to government, they have often publicly expressed their views on creativity and innovation.

Usually leaders have had something quotable to say, and some of their statements are listed below. But to bring some spice into these readings I have turned them into a "who said what?" exercise. In the list below, the quotations are attributed to the wrong persons. In the blank spaces, write the name of the person to whom each quotation should be attributed.

1. *No idea is so outlandish that it should not be considered with a searching but at the same time with a steady eye.*
   —Napoleon Bonaparte

   _____

2. *To cease to think creatively is to cease to live.*
   —Linus Pauling

   _____

3. *Originality is simply a fresh pair of eyes.*
   —William James

   _____

**4.** *To give a fair chance to potential creativity is a matter of life and death for any society.*

—Benjamin Franklin

---

**5.** *To the extent that a person makes, invents, thinks of something that is new to him, he may be said to have performed a creative act.*

—Woodrow Wilson

---

**6.** *The best way to have a good idea is to have lots of ideas.*

—Arnold Toynbee

---

**7.** *Genius, in truth, means little more than the faculty of perceiving in a habitual way.*

—Margaret Mead

---

**8.** *Imagination rules the world.*

—Winston Churchill

---

**Answers:**

1. Churchill. 2. Franklin. 3. Wilson. 4. Toynbee. 5. Mead. 6. Pauling. 7. James. 8. Napoleon.

# THE HISTORY OF CHANGE

Early attempts to solve problems and meet challenges by means of creative imagination produced simple and uncomplicated devices: spears, clubs, and swords; pots and pans; sleds, canoes, and sailboats; carts, wagons, and carriages; tunnels, bridges, and roads. When agriculture developed and villages appeared, only ten thousand years ago, plows, halters, and harnesses were designed, irrigation systems were contrived, and windmills invented.

As towns and cities grew, attention was turned to social inventions and innovations. Systems of writing and calculating were invented, as well as social institutions such as schools, churches, courts, and jails, none of which had previously existed.

Inventions were produced in the economic sphere as well: money, marketplaces, stores and shops, workshops, borrowing and lending, interest. Still other ideas were conjured up in the political realm, ideas for feudal, monarchical, oligarchic, and democratic systems and prescriptions for how each could best operate. Small wonder that H. G. Wells declared that "human history is in essence a history of ideas." Creativity and innovation transformed the world and reconstructed the human environment in technological, social, economic, political, and religious directions. Humanity even began to create another physical environment for itself—the city—superimposed upon the one provided by nature. Increasingly, this artificial environment would be where humans would spend most of their time. In sum, invention, innovation, and creativity progressively took full rein, constructing solutions to answer every human need.

Technological innovation continued. New devices were invented: the lever, the screw, the pulley. The long process of discovery and invention that led to today's astonishingly complex machines, like jets, computers, and satellites, has never stopped. Nor has the search for new and better business inventions. Think of leasing, supermarkets, hypermarkets, discount stores, rental stores, rent-to-buy stores, and franchises, or of mutual funds, junk bonds, derivatives, reverse mortgages, cash machines, credit cards, cash cards, discount stock, brokers and banking, and buying and selling on the Internet.

Innovation produces change, and change is what will make the future different from the present or past. The time continuum is one of change. Time is the dimension in which change takes place, just as space is the dimension in which motion takes place. The most exciting changes are ones that take place when something utterly new enters our world. When, in a fit of uncontrolled creative frenzy, people conjured up everything from levers, screws, and pulleys to electric lights, atomic power, jets, computers, robots, artificial intelligence, and virtual reality, they had discovered a new game: inventing the future. What fun! By imagining something impossible and seeming at times to be contrary to nature, we make ideas take form. The changes just pile up, one on top of the other, sometimes crushing those at the bottom, but often just adding to the accumulation.

Without doubt time is one of the greatest paradoxes of all. On the one hand, we say time is the great destroyer, and then we turn right around and say that time is the great healer. Time is, clearly, both things. It contains these opposites within itself.

We may cherish the past or regret it, but it's the future that means everything to us—even more than the present, which we sacrifice to small or large degree depending on how driven we are by our hopes for the future. We advise ourselves to "live for the future," work sixty hours a week, and buy as many mutual funds as we can. It is truly a paradox, nonetheless, that the future does not exist until it comes, whereas the present is real. In fact, time is nothing but an endless succession of here and nows, of presents. Just the same, it is our hopes and dreams for the future that keep us going every day.

Time is something we spend, or save, or invest. Innovators and entrepreneurs come out all the time with new products and services to save people time or help them spend it better in either leisure activities (having a good time) or self-development. These markets in time are immense, as can quickly be realized when you see all the time-related products and services available. Time is both an opportunity for profit and an opportunity to serve consumers by meeting people's time-based needs.

Only after we have looked back are we in a proper position to look forward. We know for certain the future holds endless change, endless innovation, endless creativity. It cannot be otherwise. The future will not just happen, it will be invented, just as it has been for thousands of years. It is being invented right now by millions of restless minds, entrepreneurial companies both low- and high-tech, in government laboratories, in universities and colleges, and in consulting firms, media enterprises, and the workshops of poets, artists, writers, musicians, and inventors.

Whenever a new solution has been found for a problem, the tendency has been to quickly accept its advantages but also see how limited it is. We instantly wonder whether something still better could be possible. We have gone from encasing our feet in leather, to riding a horse or elephant, to rolling on wheels, to flying on wings, and to propelling ourselves into space in rockets—all the while wondering if there are ways of traveling at the speed of light, of transmitting messages and information to distant locations in the galaxy, and of reconstituting both objects and ourselves from particles available in those distant places.

## THE FUTURE OF CHANGE

Many future developments are foreseeable, including a larger global population; continuing depletion of nonrenewable resources; a longer life span; an increasingly older population; growing tensions between conflicting cultures, ethnic groups, and religious sects; smaller and lighter autos powered by electricity or hydrogen; and more medical breakthroughs. Many other developments are unforeseeable; however it is these changes that will be greatest. They will include medical and biological breakthroughs of astonishing proportion, innovations in the criminal justice field, reconciliation of economic activity with the need to preserve the biosphere, and innovations in education, marriage, and business management. Some changes will arise from processes already at work, some will occur by accident, and some will be the result of imagination.

## THE ROLE OF LEADERSHIP

Leadership is a perennial subject, usually divided into the study of personal characteristics of leaders, relationships of leaders to their followers, and decision-making and policy-making styles. Decision making and policy formulation need an answer to these questions:

Where are we going? What do we have to do to get there? Two leading thinkers on leadership, James Kouzes and Barry Posner, suggest,
"In some ways, leaders lead their lives backwards. They see pictures
in their minds' eyes of what the results will look like even before they
have started their projects."[1] That is to say, an understanding of "reverse causality" (the intended effects produces the causes) is the basis
of leadership. Many students of leadership have come to the same
conclusion, and a whole literature exists with the purpose of getting
this message across to people in positions of authority.

Since leadership is about looking ahead, a key question is, How
far ahead? It is axiomatic that the higher in an organization or institution that a leader is, the further that leader should be looking ahead.
Omar A. el-Sawy, a student of planning, found indications that those
executives who think and plan furthest ahead are more inclined to
look back before looking forward. Ironically, executives whose minds
leap immediately to thoughts of the future look less far ahead. He calls
this the *Janus precedence effect* and explains: "The Janus precedence
effect suggests that in strategic planning sessions, if we want to plan
for the distant future, and we want the participants to elongate their
time horizons in their image of the future, let them talk about history
first. Let them look into the past and deliberate about it, before looking into the future."[2]

Sawy's findings can't help remind us of how the leaders of Japan,
defeated and destitute in 1945, set their sights on being the world's
leading economy by the year 2000. Their business leaders still look
further ahead than those of any other country in the world, and they
remain intent on building the new industries for the twenty-first century. The notoriously long time frame within which Japan's business
and political leaders plan is helped by their awareness of their country's own long history. They extend history into the distant future, to
preserve their existence and their essence, by adapting to change in a
creative and innovative manner. The Japanese example disproves the
common idea that those who look ahead, whose minds are in the future, have no interest in the past. Nor do the Japanese intend to repeat

1. James M. Kouzes and Barry Z. Posner, *The Leadership Challenge* (San Francisco:
Jossey-Bass, 1991), p. 89.
2. Omar A. el-Sawy, *Temporal Perspective and Managerial Attention: A Study of
Chief Executive Strategic Behavior.* Unpublished doctoral dissertation, Stanford
University, 1983. Quoted in ibid., p. 96.

their past mistakes. In that respect, they remind us of the observation by American philosopher George Santayana, that "those who cannot remember the past are condemned to repeat it."

The observation that those who are best at looking ahead are also good at looking back is not new. H. G. Wells, who wrote *The Time Machine, The Invisible Man*, and other pieces of futuristic fiction, spent his life looking both backward and forward. Wells was the first historian to author a history not of a single country but of the entire world. *An Outline of History* was a precedent breaker.

Leaders have to be paradoxical thinkers. As contemporary writer Gail Sheehy put it, "One common definition of leadership is the ability to keep two opposing ideas in mind at the same time and still think." Every situation for a leader is a composite of conflicting and opposing considerations, each of which is valid from a certain point of view. Each has its pros and cons, which have to be evaluated. The leader must be able to hold opposing ideas in mind and balance them judiciously. Otherwise, decisions become extremist answers with disastrous results.

The word *leader* often comes up in conversation and writing without any attempts to define it. The assumption is that we all agree on its meaning. But that is not always the case. The *leading* edge of a wing is the edge that moves forward first and cuts through the air, leading the way. The function of the leader is exactly the same. It is to lead, to be in the forefront, moving ahead while others follow. Thus we speak correctly when we say that the leader is a person who is at the leading edge or the cutting edge of their field.

## The Leader's Time Trip

In earlier days, leaders led their followers to new and better hunting grounds. Leaders still perform that function, leading their followers toward something new and better than the present situation in their industry, society, or profession. The common denominator of all leadership is movement. Leaders take us from where we are now to someplace new.

Leaders are always on a time trip, moving out of the past, through the present, and into the future. They are steered by images and visions, but they inhabit a world of fact. Vision and reality can approximate each other, but they can never coincide. Leaders may have their feet on the ground, but the future they travel to exists in their imagination. When leaders arrive at the future, they find it abruptly metamorphosed into the present.

The future exists only in the leader's mind because once it is reached, it becomes the present. Dream as much as they want about the future, it is destined one day to become their past.

The past and future, while opposites, constitute an indivisible continuum—the continuum of time. Leaders have a keen sense of the flow of time and see unity in its opposites, with the present as the link. Leaders cannot change the past. And it is too late to change the present because it is already here. But it's not too late to change the future. Unlike the past and the present, it never goes away. It can be created and shaped to fit our hopes, dreams, and possibilities. It is the leader's role to do that.

If there is a single way in which leaders are different from non-leaders, it's in how they treat time. Many people, particularly the mentally incompetent, look only a few days ahead at a time, or even only a few hours. They neither save nor plan. As a result, they get into trouble and have to be taken care of. The average person does better, but still lives very close to the present, looking neither back nor ahead more than a few weeks or months at a time. In contrast, research in Europe has shown that senior executives look further into the future than do most other folks. The essence of leadership is to look ahead, and the further the better.

There is a huge bonus in looking ahead: It is impossible to look at the future without affecting it by the very act of doing so. Thoughts will be set in motion, they will incubate in your unconscious, and will affect your behavior. One version of this phenomenon is called the *self-fulfilling prophecy*—for example, if you think you won't ever get anywhere, you won't. If you think you will, then you just might.

## Taking the Present Seriously

At the same time as they are looking into the future, leaders never forget that future actions must be built on actions taken in the present. Make sure that construction of the new plant is going full steam ahead right now. Treat your customers well every day, pay attention to what they say when they say it, and they will come back tomorrow. Leaders are action oriented; they know there is no time like the present.

Clearly, leaders must have a sense of concern and urgency about the present. There are always things that must be done right away. But they also know that acting in the present is not enough. While dealing with the urgency of present matters, they must visualize and create the future.

The leader who does not know how to delegate, how to free up time, is lost. For years I have given workshop participants a fifteen-minute freeing-up exercise. Try it yourself. On the left-hand side of a blank sheet of paper, list fifteen tasks that you regularly perform in your work. Do it with as little thinking as possible and as fast as you can. Now, examine each task to see if some can be eliminated easily—usually there are some. (It's amazing how often we complain we don't have time, and then immediately use it up thoughtlessly by doing things that need not be done at all.) Look at the tasks that are left. Put a mark against those that your direct reports could do partly or entirely. Each time you find something to assign or delegate, note down the time it will save you, even if it's only fifteen minutes a week. Then add up how many hours a week you will be able to free up for work on creative, long-term projects. The average savings managers have made after doing this exercise is a quite surprising eight hours a week.

## Past vs. Future

There are no greater opposites than past and future. Below is a list of the ways in which they are opposite, and how we relate to each of them.

| The Past | The Future |
|----------|------------|
| Behind | Ahead |
| Known | Unknown |
| Familiar | Unfamiliar |
| Certain | Uncertain |
| Closed | Open |
| Facts | Possibilities |
| Unmanageable | Manageable |
| Memories | Visions |
| Records | Scenarios |

## How to Look Backward and Forward

An innovative company in Montreal, always on the lookout for new products, had the happy thought one day of looking back through all its product failures. It turned out that several of those scrapped products were just what was needed at present. All that had been wrong was that they had been produced before the time was ripe. Forward-thinking leaders are always looking back. They search for forgotten solutions, useful perspectives, and mistakes made. How can you do a better job of exploring the past?

Books are one way. Anyone who has taken the trouble in the last decade to read *Today and Tomorrow* by Henry Ford has learned everything there is to know about process improvement and total, stem-to-gudgeon business reengineering. He said it all, and he said it clearly. Ford may be an American icon, but few know the extent of his genius because managers and management consultants rarely read what he wrote. Instead, the things Ford knew and did have to be rediscovered every ten years. The same is true of almost all the "new" management theories that crowd the bookshelves. Today's management culture ignores the past and pays the price by having to perpetually reinvent the wheel. Norman Cousins, the late editor of *Saturday Review*, described our generation as immersed in what he called "presentism," a mental aberration caused by living only in the present with little sense of the past or the future, and without any mental connection with what was and what will be.

Here are a few guidelines for exploring the past.

1. Read biographies and autobiographies of past leaders in business, science, technology, government, and the arts.
2. Visit museums of technology and industry.
3. Look at videos of film classics like Red Skelton in *The Fuller Brush Man*, William Holden in *Executive Suite*; or Charlie Chaplin in *Modern Times*.
4. Chat with some of your company's oldest employees, assuming there are some left who are significantly older.
5. Read the older management literature—brilliant books like *Functions of the Executive*, written by Chester Barnard in 1948 when he was CEO of the New Jersey Bell Telephone Company.

And when they look forward, leaders have three things firmly fixed in their heads: Leadership is moving ahead. Leadership is being ahead. Leadership is looking ahead. As a leader, you have several ways to help yourself look a good distance ahead.

1. Subscribe to publications about the future, such as *The Futurist*, a publication of the World Future Society, headquartered in Washington, D.C.
2. Read a couple of books each year that deal with important trends, shifts, and changes in demographics, the economy, technology, and society.
3. Attend several meetings each year where trends and changes in your industry or your profession are discussed.
4. Spend time with people who share your curiosity and interest in the future.

## HELPING OTHERS TO LOOK AHEAD

The challenge of companies and leaders is to navigate the time trip successfully. These days, the waters are white with the rapids of change. Challenges and problems are great, but the tools are more readily available than ever before, while alternative routes are more numerous.

One of a leader's basic responsibilities is to encourage colleagues to look ahead. You can help them by having them participate in your own process of looking ahead, soliciting their ideas on the market and the industry. If you do this regularly, they will soon have ideas to provide, and you will be pleased with these thoughts and ideas.

Hold daylong blue-sky meetings each quarter with your top twenty or thirty people, including your direct reports. In the meeting, have presentations and small-group discussions of technological, economic, and geopolitical trends. Provide participants with futurist articles and reports to read beforehand. Hand out copies of the bestseller futurist books, of which there are always one or two in bookstores at any time. Hold these meetings anywhere but on your own premises. There is something about the mere presence of a corporate building that holds the mind in the firm grasp of the here and now. In the new management world, it takes a team of executives working together to discern the opportunities and challenges opening up. So explore these strategic issues in an environment free of time pressures.

## Matrix Analysis for Strategic Planning and Innovation

The subject of how to plan, organize, and conduct strategy sessions is outside the scope of the present book. However, we recently developed a tool that has been found useful by our clients at such meetings, and it is shown in the accompanying figure. We call it a Matrix Analysis for Strategic Planning and Innovation.

| | Environmental Changes | | | |
| --- | --- | --- | --- | --- |
| | Social | Economic | Political | Technologic |
| | | | | |
| | | | | |
| | | | | |
| new products or services | | | | |
| new marketing innovations | | | | |
| organization and management innovations | | | | |
| new employee relations concepts | | | | |

The idea is that each participant spends ten minutes jotting down a few words in each box, reflecting what he or she may be thinking.

For example, with regard to strategic environmental change in the economic environment, a participant may think of Latin America; having done so, he will jot the words "Latin America" down on the uppermost box under the heading "Economic." Each participant goes through the matrix, filling in as many items as come to mind with respect to social, economic, political, and economic changes.

Suppose that one-fourth or more of the group has identified Latin America on the matrix. That should be enough to justify an exploration of Latin American developments and changes. The facilitator of the meeting then guides discussion of the various environmental changes that have been flagged by participants with respect to three new products and services, three new marketing policies and practices, three possible innovations in the company's management methods, and three innovations in employee relations policies and practices.

Depending on the time available, the group might turn to a social change occurring closer to home and explore, in similar fashion, its implications for strategic innovations and initiatives the company could take in response to that change. Obviously, there is no shortage of social changes to examine for strategic significance.

## Looking Back From the Future

There is a clever trick of the mind that can be used for visualizing the future: pretend that the future is already here. Try it first on your personal future, imagining it's ten years from now. Where are you? What is your life like? Fantasize about it for a minute or two. How old are you and your spouse? You are living in another country and city. What work are you doing? How's your health? How old are your children? What are they doing for a living? What is the total value of your net assets, corrected for inflation? How much is in real estate, stocks and bonds, pension plan equity, and personal valuables? What about your life do you like? Now go back to the present. What can you do about any of what lies ahead of you if you start working at it right now?

The trick of looking backward from the future was one that Merlin, the magician in King Arthur's court, was able to do instinctively. In T. H. White's book *The Once and Future King,* he has Merlin say to King Arthur, who was always surprised at Merlin's presence, "Ah, yes. How did I know to set breakfast for two? . . . Now ordinary people are born forwards in Time, if you understand what I mean, and nearly everything in the world goes forward too. This makes it quite easy for ordinary people to live. . . . But unfortunately I was born at the wrong end of time, and I have to live backwards from in front, while surrounded by a lot of people living forward from behind.[3]

However, Merlin was wrong—in one respect. We ordinary people can also, if we want to, live backward from the future. Our minds and brains are endowed with the imagination and foresight that enables us to visualize ourselves at some future point in time and look backward from it to the present. It is an ability that we could easily utilize more often than we do. By adopting Merlin's trick we can, to some degree, look back to see our lives with more understanding, better ready to know what to expect.

In this same way, corporate futures can be made controllable in some respects even while they remain uncontrollable in others. A business leader can have a lot more decision control than imagined. For instance, I sometimes ask middle management people which of them believe they could decide to live and work in some other country if they wanted to and be pretty sure to be there within three years. Almost everyone says they could do just that if they cared to make the change. Indeed, most of us can alter our futures to a much greater degree than we appreciate.

Do a similar thing with your business as you did earlier about your personal life: What will things be like ten years from now? Put the question on the agenda of your next blue-sky meeting. Before the meeting, have participants do some research and some conventional looking ahead. Give each a different question, then at the meeting ask what has come to pass, what it all has meant to the world.

For example, what is the world's supply of fuel for energy and heat? What is the population of the world likely to be? (It was nearly 6 billion by 1996, and growing rapidly.) What is the condition of the world's supply of arable land, fish, iron ore, nickel? What country has the highest standard of living? Country by country, what percentage of the population is over sixty? What percentage is under twenty? What are the three largest industries? What percentage of CEOs are women? What percentage of the population are engineers, architects, and scientists?

3. T. H. White, *The Once and Future King* (Garden City, N.Y.: Doubleday, Page and Company, 1926).

# THE DIALECTICAL DANCE

In Chapter 4, I noted that the importance of opposites has been observed for millennia, starting with Heraclitus in Greece and Lao-tzu in China around 450 B.C. This continues with Hegel, Darwin, and Marx in the nineteenth century, and carries on with still other thinkers to this very day. There are ways to handle the jousting and reconciliation that take place between opposites. Creative leaders can take advantage of this dialectic, the strategic value of which is measured in millions of dollars in revenues. The changing patterns produced by the flow of opposites in the business environment have identifiable implications for management styles as well as marketing and sales. A quick scan of some classical views of the subject can help set the stage for further reflection.

For Heraclitus, the continual conflict between opposites meant that we live in a world in which ideas, institutions, and even the elements wage perpetual battle for dominance. Strife and conflict are the normal state of affairs; peace, calm, and harmony are only interludes. Heraclitus considered himself a realist; those who could not see this strife between opposites were self-deluded fools. His view made him few friends and obtained little approval, but Heraclitus was not a person to care much about what others thought of him.

If Heraclitus were alive today, he would cite as examples of his view the conflicts between liberalism and conservatism, the arguments between pro-lifers and right-to-lifers, the tensions between dark-colored and light-colored social groups, the battles between the sexes and between the young and the old, the disputes between consumerism and conservation, the deepening divisions between rich and poor, the everlasting differences between organized labor and management, and the wars between competing corporations for market hegemony.

This jousting for position sculpts the world and our society accepts it as valid. Opposites act as chisels that shape our social, economic, and political reality. Astute leaders never take their eyes from the battle of the opposites, waiting for the threats or opportunities that will arise from it.

In management circles, seesaw change is reflected in the way concepts of centralization and decentralization vie for popularity, one popular for a few years only to be replaced temporarily by the other. Creative managers know how to employ philosophies both simultaneously, in a balanced and integrated manner. With the passage of time, things do change and old concepts and practices become better; the world renews itself in many ways.

Edith Weiner, president of the New York City management consulting firm Weiner, Edrich, Brown, speaks frequently about how opposite trends interplay. She describes market change as an ongoing dialectic between consumer trends and consumer countertrends. A countertrend emerges as a response to some trend that already exists. For example, the trend toward high technology and wired connectedness via fax, modem, Internet, cellular phone, and teleconferencing prompted the countertrend toward escapes to island cottages, meditation rooms, gardens, spices, perfumes, natural foods, and old-fashioned holidays. Trends and countertrends coexist, even marry. Designer jeans mesh the desire to express status with the desire to wear rugged, casual clothing. What is more paradoxical?

Consciousness of the dialectical nature of change gives the strategist and leader a leg up that others lack. If there is a boom in mutual funds and a decline in investing in housing, be sure that somewhere in the economy there are people moving in the opposite direction, deciding that now is just the right time to buy a bigger or more expensive house. If people have been buying bigger houses, somewhere there is a nascent movement toward smaller houses.

The existing trend toward more years of formal education keeps people from beginning their careers until their late twenties. This may already be seeding an era where people skip formal education and get on with life at an earlier age. Thus, as more people go to school, more people stay away, but the people who stay away become a giant market for do-it-yourself computer and video learning programs. It's not that they don't want knowledge, it's that they want knowledge and income to flow in at the same time—Janusian thinking. Remember that when things are going in one direction, somewhere they are going in the opposite direction.

## Inventing the Future for Your Company

Inventing the future is totally different from predicting it or planning and controlling it. Companies have to elicit from everyone in the organization the motivation and energy it takes to be innovative and successful. The following what to do's cover a broad range. Put a check mark next to any that you are already doing or intend to do.

☐ Organize "looking back" sessions for the company, by department and unit, to see where the company is coming from. List what the past can teach, in the form of mistakes that were made, lessons that were learned, and valuable things the company once knew but has forgotten.

☐ Scan the environment globally and locally for changes that spell corporate opportunities or problems, including changes that initially seem to have nothing at all to do with the business.

☐ Visualize alternative, quite opposite, and wholly new directions in which the company can go by exploiting its innovative capabilities.

☐ Incorporate innovative visions, goals, and objectives into the strategic planning process. Go to the bottom of the organization to get ideas before you go to the top.

☐ Structure a framework for innovative initiatives by setting up strategic business units and such entrepreneurial entities as new business incubators and hatcheries.

☐ Introduce innovation-based reward systems of both nonfinancial and financial natures. Make high-level performance a basic requirement for keeping the job, and give bonuses only for innovative achievements. Promote only persons who have brought about important innovations.

☐ Examine the corporate culture for counterinnovative values, beliefs, customs, codes, norms, habits, and procedures. Plan how to substitute better cultural elements.

☐ Review the corporate atmosphere for counterinnovative patterns of feeling, miscommunication, conflict, poor coordination, suspicions, hostilities, silent wars. Move these corporate atmospherics in the opposite direction, toward openness, trust, freedom of expression, and mutual caring. Use modern OD (organization development) methods to do this.

☐ Teach paradoxical thinking and creativity, stressing contrarian, Janusian, and Hegelian thinking. Teach everyone how to organize and manage creativity teams.

☐ Provide think-tank rooms and residential facilities where creativity teams can repair to for a few hours, a few days, or a few weeks at a time.

☐ Examine the management process for such counterinnovative characteristics as being tradition driven, inward looking, or overobsessed with routines and procedures, preoccupied with activities rather than results, engaged in top-down direction and control, given to individualistic self-serving modes of managing and working rather than Hegelian-type teamwork.

☐ Develop a fully functioning, future-focused, outward-looking, innovatory, goal-oriented, results-seeking, participatory and teamwork management process.

The 3M Company has a name synonymous with innovation. Its whole product line consists of its own invention. According to David Sorensen, executive director of 3M's Corporate Technical Planning and Coordination Department, 3M is a company where the idea of paradox holds sway, and where trend and countertrend are both acknowledged.

> Today, neither big nor small is either beautiful or bad. The correct answer is, It all depends. Whether we approach customers on a macro or a micro scale, there is one constant. Within our structure, we organize to work small, either by establishing tiny business units or forming truly independent teams within large organizations. In either case, the unit or team is able to concentrate on its own idea, technology, or product. This approach helps us to achieve the seemingly contradictory goals of being large and small simultaneously.[4]

## A SUMMARIZING PERSPECTIVE

The drama of creativity and change is played out on a time axis, requiring business leaders to be constantly looking both backward and forward in their effort to be ahead and stay ahead. Examples abound of creative, time-conscious leaders with a happy acceptance and ingenious aptitude for paradoxical thinking. Real leaders have always by instinct engaged in the behavior we call the Paradox Process. They have been totally committed to constructive change through creativity and innovation. Now, education in the Paradox Process can be a useful part of your management approach and you can foster paradoxical thinking in your employees as well.

4. David P. Sorensen, *Innovations: Key to Business Success* (Menlo Park, Calif.: Crisp Publications, 1997), p. 20.

# Chapter 8

# CREATIVE THINKING: CHARACTERISTICS AND SKILLS

"Imagination is more important than knowledge."

—Albert Einstein

Paradoxical thinking cannot be separated from the overall process of creative thought. It is creative thinking that drives the Paradox Process. This chapter, therefore, analyzes creative thinking, looks at how it functions, and helps you sharpen your skills in the advanced cognitive processes of perception, intuition, imagination, and paradox.

Gardner Kent's creative breakthrough for his Green Tortoise bus line, described in Chapter 3, followed a pattern quite common for such innovations, identified over sixty years ago by a researcher named Graham Wallas. Wallas carried out systematic analyses of people who had made important breakthroughs in various fields.[1] He discovered that all these individuals passed through the same four stages.

In the first stage, there had been conscious work on the project in question, work that entailed lot of floundering around with little or no apparent headway made. In fact, this was a necessary period of preparation for the mind, without which it had nothing to draw from. There followed a second period, described as "incubation," when

1. Graham Wallas, *The Art of Thought* (New York: Harcourt Brace, 1926).

nothing was done consciously to solve the problem. Then, an experience of "illumination" would occur, as if a light had been turned on. The answer leapt into view in a eurekalike flash of insight. Finally, the insight was checked by critical examination, experimentation, and testing. The incubation period was not quite as inactive as it appeared. In actuality, the brain had been working at an unconscious level.

Thus, according to Wallas, the four stages in breakthrough thinking are (1) preparation, (2) incubation, (3) illumination, and (4) testing. Keep in mind that there are two important stages—conscious work and incubation—that have to occur before illumination and discovery can happen. When you are working at a problem and the answer is not coming, you tell yourself to put it on the back burner. Consciously anticipate these four stages and be ready to go through them deliberately.

In practice, the process is more complicated because these stages overlap. For example, mini-breakthroughs may occur as you go along, each one readying the stage for the next, until all becomes clear. In addition, you may be collecting new information and analyzing it at the same time as certain subsidiary ideas are incubating. When you are not thinking consciously of your problem, you nevertheless continue to pick up relevant information.

## THE EUREKA PHENOMENON

Creative insights often come to us seemingly out of the blue. The classic illustration of sudden insight is from the ancient Greeks. Archimedes had been asked to find out whether a crown that had been given to the king was pure gold or a cheap amalgam. Knowing its weight relative to its volume would provide the answer. The weight could be easily established by using a scale. But how could he measure the volume of something as filigreed and complex as a crown? Archimedes was stumped.

For quite a few days he racked his brains, getting nowhere. Then, one day, as Archimedes was seating himself in his bath and the water rose as he settled into it, the answer struck him like a bolt out of the blue. If he were to set the crown into the bath instead of himself, the water would also rise an amount equal to the volume of the crown. Knowing the weight and volume of the crown, he could calculate its weight per unit of volume and establish immediately whether it was heavier, lighter, or the same as one made of pure gold. In his excitement at this sudden illumination, Archimedes shouted "Eureka"—Greek, of course, for "I have found it."

Today our cartoons show individuals with imaginary light bulbs over their heads to show a sudden insight. The eureka experience is indeed very much that of having a light turned on. The answer seems so clear and certain, we say to ourselves in puzzlement, "Why didn't I see it sooner?" Or "I could kick myself for not seeing this sooner." The reason is that the answer simply was not in your brain to be seen until that point.

## BREAKTHROUGHS ARE EXACTLY THAT

Sudden insights and new discoveries provide us with what we call a breakthrough. We speak of "a new medical breakthrough," "a breakthrough discovery," "a breakthrough idea."

The word *breakthrough* is, of course, a metaphor, conjuring up the image of surmounting an insurmountable obstacle—a wall that seemed too high. Breakthroughs are accomplished by dint of persistent force and simple trial and error. When a breakthrough happens, it is unexpected, always a bit of a startle.

The creative process is characterized by both small and large breakthroughs. You want a solution, you want to move ahead, you are convinced there is an answer. But it feels as if you are on one side of a wall and the answer is on the other side. The wall has to be broken through. The breakthrough metaphor is therefore apt. It resonates with everything we see, hear, and experience in the creative process.

The breakthrough metaphor also invites the question of what these barriers really are and where they come from. Many are within ourselves. Some are preconceptions or prejudices. Others may come from an unconscious desire to achieve consensus. Some stem from a reluctance to let our minds entertain fanciful ideas, others from reluctance to admit that existing solutions won't work. Some come from a wish to avoid the floundering around, the confusion, perplexity, and frustration that creativity entails. Pushing away the obstacles that you've set up for yourself is an important step toward finding a solution. If you are having trouble with a problem, don't look only at it; look at yourself as well.

## Our Cognitive Processes

The human mind is equipped with powerful capabilities for producing solutions, breakthroughs, and innovations. The more you know about those capabilities, the better position you are in to take advantage of them.

These creative thinking processes go beyond those used in common sense and everyday reasoning. Nonetheless, the creative thinking processes also make use of memory, logic, reason, and judgment. Otherwise, the mind would produce only fantasies, delusions, superstitions, self-deceptions, and crackpot solutions to real-world problems. The basic skills keep us in touch with reality. Indeed, without the reality checks provided by the basic cognitive processes, there's no innovation.

The chief danger to the progress of innovation, however, is that the creative thinking skills are those most often neglected. It's a long tradition in our schools to emphasize memory, logic, reason, and judgment. Extolling the virtues of these basic cognitive skills began when Aristotle dubbed humans as "the rational animal." It continued into the eighteenth century and the Age of Reason, and persists to the present. It reaches its zenith with the conviction that the ability to manipulate facts in a systematic manner is the chief thinking skill of the human being. This notion stands as one of the greatest errors of all time.

When the basic cognitive skills aren't enough, we may be forced to become inventive and really put our minds to work. We see opportunities that didn't exist before, or problems never before experienced, and we have to create answers out of whole cloth. We have to be ingenious, inventive, creative, and innovative. At that point, a whole battery of higher-level cognitive resources come into play. These higher processes include perception, intuition, paradoxical thinking, and imagination. To make your breakthrough, you may need to employ one, two, or all three of them.

## The Unconscious Mind

The mind keeps thinking, whether we are aware it is doing so or not. It thinks all day long, and all night long, too. When we are awake, the mind thinks about some matter, or even several of them, at the same time it is giving attention to another. You may be working on your income tax, but part of your mind is sorting out a sales problem you have at the office and another part is incubating plans for your next ski trip. Unlike the former U.S. president who was accused of not being able to walk and chew gum at the same time, the mind can do a dozen or more things simultaneously, some of them consciously and others subconsciously.

We can no more see all that is going on in our brains than we can see what is going on in our desktop computers. William Lear, inventor of the Lear Jet, would pour ideas out in a torrent. He was once asked what message he would give schools, based on his demonstrated successes as a creative thinker. Lear said they should stop teaching children how to think consciously and start teaching them how to think unconsciously.

Creative thinking occurs at unconscious as well as conscious levels, albeit in response to inputs mostly (but not entirely) at a conscious level. Both conscious and unconscious thinking work in a back-and-forth sequence to produce breakthroughs. The four stages of the creative process—preparation, incubation, illumination, and testing—confirm that much important thinking goes on when we are not aware. In fact, it is most often the unconscious mind that produces the creative answers our conscious mind is asking for. The conscious mind has limits that the unconscious mind does not know.

## PERCEPTION AND INTUITION

*Perception* is the mental process that helps you recognize things for what they are. You see a figure walking across a road and recognize it as your sister. You see some dishes on a kitchen table and recognize that they are dirty. The recognitions are instant. You do not have to search each detail or go through a process of logical reasoning to conclude that the figure is your sister or the dishes are dirty. Perception gives you a pattern. It is that pattern that perception recognizes, not the details. The pattern is all you need; it's the forest rather than the trees.

However, if what you see is unclear or obscured, recognition may not be immediate. The weather could be drizzly and your sister half hidden under an umbrella. Then it takes you several seconds before you recognize her. Perceiving the pattern can take even longer when the matter is something more complex. Take going to work at a new job. In the beginning, nothing is clear. Slowly, a few things become clear, then a few more. It may be weeks or longer before you discover the overall pattern of things, and the pieces fall together.

At times, *intuition* can be more penetrating than perception. Intuition is similar to perception in many ways, except that it involves deeper levels of the mind. It is also sometimes less reliable than perception. Intuition is the act or faculty of knowing something directly without the use of intervening rational processes. The word is derived from the Latin *intuēri*, which means "to look at." *Intuition* is a word we use when we know something but can't explain how we know it. Sometimes intuition is weak and uncertain, in which case we say we have a "hunch" or "a feeling." At other times, it is strong and confident and provides us (we believe) with powerful insights into a situation, a problem, or an aspect of human behavior.

Modern cognitive psychology offers no convincing explanation for how the brain makes intuition possible, but there is no doubt that it is important. Almost all great geniuses in business, finance, science, or politics say they rely heavily on it. The ancients, also aware of its presence and importance, attributed it to a third eye buried deep inside the brain. This third eye supposedly enabled humans to see more penetratingly into the hidden nature of complex issues and situations, and to have insights into everyday puzzles as well. Here are some examples:

• Your son has been acting a little different from the way he usually does, but you can't put your finger on it. That and an odd remark make you sense that something at school is troubling him. You are not surprised when you find your intuition was right.

• You suspect that one of your colleagues is untrustworthy.

Again, there's nothing you can put your finger on. But you are not as surprised as you might have been when you learn he has pulled a dirty trick on someone you know. Your intuition was right.

• You sense that one of your suppliers is drifting into serious difficulties. It's something in the tone of voice of their people, something in the way they do not respond to complaints they used to take seriously. Your intuition turns out to be right. The service goes from bad to worse, and you turn to another supplier. In fact, your intuition was strong enough that you had already started to think of alternative suppliers.

During the creative process, you may confront one of several different conditions at the beginning:

1. You see the situation clearly—there is a clear pattern and all you need is a solution. If a good solution is available, you can use it. If you want a better solution, you can invent it.

2. You do not see the situation clearly—it is ambiguous and if there is a pattern, you do not see it. You can keep looking and a pattern may eventually become clear.

3. If a solution does exist but no one has it, you will have to search yourself. Often the solution is there but no one has seen it.

4. If a solution does not exist, it has to be invented. Your imagination has to get to work.

To experience how those lights can go on and illuminate a solution, look at the picture on the next page. Normally, you won't see anything at first, but keep trying. If the picture doesn't leap out at you after a minute or two, ask a friend if he or she can see it. If you give up, the answer is shown upside down under the diagram.

**Answer:**

The picture shows a dalmatian sniffing at a spot on the ground.

## Pattern Perception

Finding a solution is often a matter of perceiving a pattern or phenomenon that you had not seen before. A legendary story of pattern perception involves the famous mathematician Carl Friedrich
Gauss. When he was a small boy in grade school, his teacher had
been writing numbers on the blackboard that the children had to
add, multiply, or divide. When they had done the work and gotten
their answers, they would be called upon to recite them. The
teacher had written down numbers to be added: 1,2,3,4,5,6,7,8,
9,10. Gauss had the answer instantly and called out "Fifty-five!"

How could he have gotten it so fast? the teacher asked. The

young Gauss explained that he had noticed right away that there was a symmetrical pattern to the numbers. One and 10 made 11; 2 and 9 made 11; 8 and 3 made 11; 7 and 4 made 11, and 5 and 6 made 11. Since there were five symmetrical pairs, the total was 55.

Genius has often been defined as the ability to look at what everyone has looked at before but see things that no one has seen before. It is interesting that Gauss looked first at the opposite ends of the series and saw that they added to 11. What instinct caused him to do this can't be said for sure, but in singling out opposites he showed one of the dominant traits of creative action.

Granted that Gauss was a genius, his solution raises a question: Can you do a better job of finding solutions if you know that they involve perceiving patterns staring you in the face? Can you move yourself a notch or two closer to genius? Yes. We do not normally see all the patterns in a situation, but these patterns are there. If you keep looking, you will likely find them.

For example, a physician may discover a pattern of occurrence in an illness. Suppose the doctor had many older patients with knee problems. She makes it her business to learn more about knee problems and their treatment. Eventually she sees a few patterns. For example, the knee-problem patients are often overweight, eat the wrong foods, and don't exercise. Seeing this pattern, she can prescribe appropriate treatment.

A computer retailer notices that older customers buy more game software than middle-aged customers and that the games they prefer are different, so he stocks the appropriate games for them.

Some physicians and retailers are as curious as those in these two examples, but many are not. As it says in Psalms (115:5-6) "Eyes have they, but they see not. They have ears, but they hear not." It would obviously pay people to become more curious about such patterns. If schools and colleges do not teach these skills of perception, companies and professional associations can. We can certainly teach them to ourselves.

## Searching for Patterns

There is always more to any situation than first meets the eye. The following problem will enable you to experience the process of finding and recognizing patterns. The diagram on the next page contains a number of squares. When I ask my workshop groups how many squares there are, almost everyone instantly sees a large square and sixteen smaller squares within it, making a total of seventeen squares. How many squares can you find?

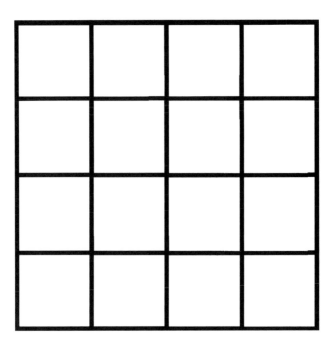

Nobody ever sees more than these seventeen squares—until I ask them to look further. After all, why bother? There is no obvious reason to look for more. But when I ask them to find more, they do look, thinking I may have a reason. Most people then find four more squares. Can you?

The next diagram indicates where these four squares are located. They are larger squares, each consisting of four smaller squares.

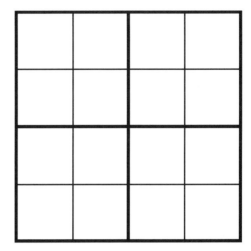

Almost simultaneously, other people see an additional five, as shown in the diagrams below:

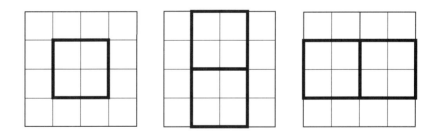

The number of squares has now jumped from seventeen to twenty-six. A little extra looking, and a lot more get seen. The participants keep looking but see no more. Then suddenly someone pipes up, a bit surprised. "I see four more, but they're different four squares each made up of nine of the small squares."

What is discerned is indicated in the following diagrams. The total is now up to thirty, almost double the seventeen squares originally seen. But from now on, the going gets tougher. Finding more squares may be difficult.

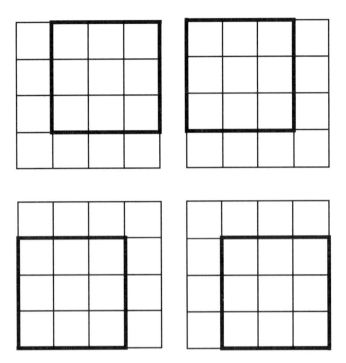

Are there any more squares? Maybe not—after all, how many can there possibly be? Some participants start to make mathematical calculations, looking for a formula that would give them the total number of squares. But there is no such formula, nor can there ever be. Since they are busy with pencil and paper, they stop looking at the diagram, which is the only place where they can find squares.

Often, someone makes a breakthrough and exclaims, "There are a total of sixty squares—thirty white squares and thirty black squares." Eureka! But this starts a debate: What is a square? Some say the black lines are what constitute the squares; others say the white areas are squares in and of themselves. The consensus is that there are two kinds of squares—the black and the white—and they just happen to coexist in this diagram.

A further breakthrough occurs: Someone reports that there are twenty-five small, darker looking squares at the intersections where the thick black lines meet. Now we're up to eighty-five squares, a very far cry from the original seventeen. There is a demand from the group for a final answer: How many squares are there? I have to answer, "I don't know."

In the workshops, we look at the diagram projected on an overhead screen. If I turn the slide over and we look at its other side, are these the same eighty-five squares or an additional eighty-five? Or again, the boundaries where the black squares meet the white squares are square boundaries. Do we count these boundaries as squares? Someone points out that we may be looking at the front of a large cube that is divided into 256 smaller cubes. By now, everyone has forgotten that only seventeen squares had been seen initially. There is some discomfort with the idea that the answers have become progressively ambiguous.

## Divergent and Convergent Thinking

Exploring a wide front for as many patterns, ideas, and possibilities as you have time to find is called *divergent thinking*. You do this when you scout a new site for a factory or office. You certainly do it when you recruit a new senior executive.

At a certain point in the search process, you discover there are a few attractive options, and then you start in the opposite direction—you enter into a thinking process called *convergent thinking*. You begin to narrow the search down to a few possibilities and then select one. At that point you move from thought to action and you negotiate a contract. Sometimes luck strikes quickly and the divergent exploration is terminated almost before it's begun because you have chanced into exactly what you want.

The more divergent thinking you do, within limits, the greater are your chances of finding the best plant, office, or executive. This applies to everything you do. If you want to come up with an outstanding advertising strategy, the wider your search and the more possibilities you look at, the greater the chances you'll end up with a winner. But you have to be both willing and able to take enough time, because the process is not fast.

In our action-oriented environment, there is always a temptation to shorten the divergent thinking process—"cut to the chase," decide, act. People who make up their minds quickly are rarely criticized for it, while people who explore before acting are often seen as indecisive and possibly weak. In this psychological milieu there is always the risk that alternative possibilities have not been sufficiently explored.

When Herbert Smith took over as president of General Electric Canada, he found some vice-presidents asking him for authorization to make million-dollar expenditures. The requests were buttressed with details on how the money would be spent and why. But when he asked what alternatives had been considered, the vice-presidents looked at him blankly—obviously not having considered any at all, so satisfied were they with what they were proposing. He would say, "This expenditure is justifiable as you have shown, but I will not authorize it unless you can tell me why it is better than some alternatives you have also examined." When they came back, he would then automatically authorize the original proposal or some better idea they had come up with. He was teaching them the importance of divergent thinking. It was not long, of course, before divergent thinking became common practice for all important decisions in this company.

In divergent thinking, you let your mind go outward, away from the problem or question, rather than directly toward it. If asked what pencils are for, convergent thinkers say only "to write." But divergent thinkers will say "to throw," "to chew," "to make small spears with," "to use as kindling," "to make rafts for white mice," and so on. Divergent thinking is broad, exploratory, and mind expanding; convergent thinking is narrow, focused, and concentrated. Both are good and both must be used. Divergent thinking is the activity of your mind when it searches into the possible rather than the actual. It plays with ideas and conjectures in a playful way and leaves the serious acts of choice and action to the convergent thinking of the mind.

Our traditional managerial culture is enormously biased toward convergent thinking. As managers, professionals, and employees become more innovative and entrepreneurial, however, they begin to redress the imbalance between divergent and convergent thinking.

## Serendipity

An interesting thing happens during divergent thinking: You come across things that you had not noticed before. When you walk across Times Square, practically every face is new. You never saw these people before and never will see them again. But if you are a photographer, some of these faces would seize your attention. If you were a panhandler, you'd spot some fair prospects.

Chance is always at work. Invariably, you luck in to something you didn't plan and didn't expect. If the things we lucked in to were rarely of any importance, there would be no reason to bring this up. But the truth is that some of the most important things in life are simply lucked in to. The role that chance plays in our personal, professional, and business destinies is nothing less than enormous.

The role of chance and luck in innovation is also enormous, almost unbelievably so. George Westinghouse stumbled across the idea of pneumatic power while reading an article in a Scout magazine. The article told of the pneumatic drills and hammers used to break rock in the construction of tunnels in the Swiss Alps. In this case, it seems there was no period of incubation. The idea came to him instantly that pneumatic power could be used for braking trains, and the Westinghouse air brake was on its way.

One of my client companies discovered an opportunity to sell newsprint in Brazil during a luncheon meeting on an entirely different matter. The company had had no clients in Brazil; now it has not only the one discovered by accident but several others as well.

James Schlatter of G.D. Searle and Company was trying to mix some amino acids to come up with a test for an ulcer drug. Some of the mixture got on his fingers. When he licked it off, it tasted sweet: He had discovered the artificial sweetener aspartame. Within three years, aspartame accounted for 70 percent of the company's profits.

A legendary case of serendipity was the discovery of 3M's Post-it notes. They sell by the billions, and use an adhesive developed by 3M's Spencer Silver. The adhesive started life as a bungle, ridiculed when it first appeared because it wouldn't stick properly. Some wits lampooned it as an "unglue." It was the opposite of what they had been aiming at and an embarrassment to Silver. But one day a colleague of Silver's named Art Fry, a steady churchgoer, found that his little paper notes kept falling from his hymnbook. It hit him that Dr. Silver's unglue was just what he needed. Talk about divine inspiration. He could stick the notes temporarily onto the book and remove them easily after they'd served their purpose. The unglue would hold the notes firmly but temporarily.

Examples of serendipity are endless. These creative break-throughs are not merely impressive, they are staggering. Yet serendipity happens only to people who are exploring, who are on the lookout as they wander off the beaten path. The word *serendipity* is found in a book by Horace Walpole, called *The Three Princes of Serendip*. Serendip was the country now known as Sri Lanka. In the tale, three princes were sent out in different directions to travel the world, and the book tells of all the fortuitous adventures, marvels, and prizes they encountered. Experienced entrepreneurs and innovators know that, like these princes, they will encounter serendipitous opportunities as often as they will those they plan for. Keeping this in mind, is there any way to make more happy accidents happen? Yes.

1. The more you explore, the more often chance events will happen—so do more exploring.
2. Get off the beaten path as often as you can. It's untapped territory and chances may be higher there.
3. Do some things on pure whim, with no reason other than the hope that some lucky thing will be encountered. Every now and then the whim will prove to have been inspired.

## New Angles and Points of View

Ideas often come when we look at things from a different point of view. Problems often become clearer or take on a different aspect. The following diagram is as simple as can be. If you look at it just as I have drawn it, it appears to be just an irregular polygon. But tilt your head a few degrees and it leaps out at you instantly as a kite.

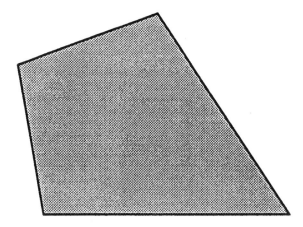

The figure below was drawn by Michelangelo in the course of his research on perspective. It is an impressive illustration of the effect of viewpoint. Move your head to the right-hand side of the page, bring it down to within a few inches of the paper, move it slowly to the side, and move it back and forth from the paper. You'll find just the right angle of view that will make the face leap out with sudden clarity. It's another piece of evidence showing the importance of looking at things from the right angle.

Looking at things from a different angle can be something you do mentally, not only physically. Anyone who wants to discover new aspects of a situation need only alter the viewpoint. Look from many different perspectives, even an opposite point of view, to get better at problem solving, seeing new opportunities, and inventing new solutions. You'll discover a larger range of possibilities.

The sketch on the next page allows you to test your willingness to entertain several possibilities in a given situation. There are no good or bad scores. Just try to see at least three different things in the drawing. Try rotating the diagram, and you may spot a few more. Following the drawing, printed upside down, are some things that people in my creativity workshops have said they could see.

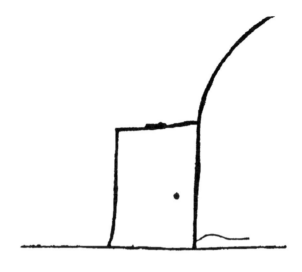

**Answers:**

tion of two roads, the entrance to an igloo seen from the side.
door, a spool of wire or thread, an aerial sketch of a lot at the intersec-
A chair with a bent back, a raggedy top hat, a chimney on a roof, a

## IMAGINATION

Breakthrough solutions come from looking for something that does not exist until someone imagines it. Can imagination precede existence? Definitely. This almost sounds like a contradiction, but it isn't—given the powers of the human mind. The brain has evolved over the millennia to the point where it has become a machine, if you will, that enables us to think about the imaginary and not only the real. Imagination is a neurological action produced by evolutionary processes for the purpose of helping us survive. It exists for primarily practical reasons.

But what is practical in imagining things that don't exist? The neural apparatus we call imagination is designed, amazingly, not just to imagine anything but to imagine things that could be made to exist. It is one of the great miracles of evolution, as long as we put it to work for us. Let's do some action research by putting imagination to work on some simple problems that only imagination can solve.

The following are several problems whose solutions come only when that light goes on, when that flash of insight shows the answer. If you solve one of these problems right now you are doing well—give yourself a bronze medal. If you get two, give yourself a silver medal; and if you get three, give yourself a gold medal and send out a press release. The answers to all three are given after the third problem.

Solving these problems requires you to employ visual imagery and imagination. Imagination simply means "making images," images in the mind's eye. To solve these problems, logic and reason won't hack it unless supported by image making.

### THE SIX COINS

Rearrange the six coins below so that they make two rows of four each.

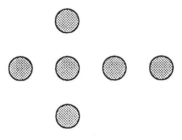

### THE SIX MATCHES

Put six wooden matches on the table or desk before you, as shown on the next page. Make an equilateral triangle from three of them. Use the remaining three matches to complete three more triangles, for a total of four. Each side of each triangle is to be the full length of a match.

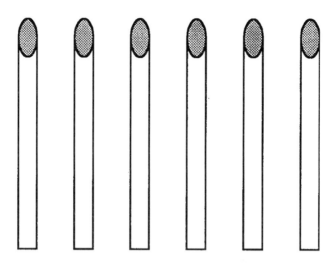

## THE MONK'S PROBLEM

One morning, exactly at sunrise, a monk began to climb a tall mountain. A narrow path no more than a foot or two wide spiraled around the mountain to a temple at the top. The monk ascended at varying rates of speed, stopping many times along the way to rest. He reached the temple shortly before sunset. After several days of fasting and meditation, he began his journey back down along the same path, starting at sunrise and again walking at variable speeds with many pauses along the way. His average speed descending was, of course, greater than his average climbing speed. Prove that there is a spot along the path that the monk will occupy on both trips and at precisely the same time of day.

**Answers and discussion:** The solution to the coins problem is to pick up the coin to the right and put it on top of the middle coin. The answer to the matches problem is to build a three-sided pyramid. The usual approach is to try to work out these problems in two dimensions right on the flat surface. It is only after a peak of frustration that a breakthrough is made and the two-dimensional is abandoned. As soon as people start imagining solutions in three dimensions, they find the answers.

What is interesting is that an image of the solution appears in the imagination before the hands reach down to move the coins or hold the matches upright to show the solution.

The solution to the monk problem calls for even more imagination. Imagine that at the same time the monk started to walk up the mountain, one of his fellow monks started walking down. No matter at what speed or with what delays the fellow monk walked down, there would be a place and a time where they would meet and pass. The only difference is that it is a fellow monk coming down, and not himself, and that it is a different day of the week. Or if it helps you better, imagine that at the moment the monk starts up the mountain, a ghost of himself starts down and previews the trip that he himself is to make the next day. There would obviously have to be a time and place where he and his ghost would pass each other.

## Playback

Perception and imagination are two mental processes that work hand in hand in producing new solutions. New solutions are sometimes discovered by direct perception or intuition, the latter being a deeper power of perception. But often, all the powers of perception in the world won't produce a solution unless imagination is called in to help. One of the most remarkable attributes of the imagination is generosity, often conjuring up not one but several solutions to a problem. Now that we have done a replay of our topic and learned some things from the previous problems, the next problem will be a piece of cake.

### THE COCKTAIL GLASS

Put four matches on a table to resemble a cocktail glass, as in the following drawing. Put a button or something like that in the glass to represent a cherry. (Sorry, the glass has no base to stand on.) Move only two matches so that the cherry ends up outside the glass. Three possible solutions follow, but you may come up with one that no one else has.

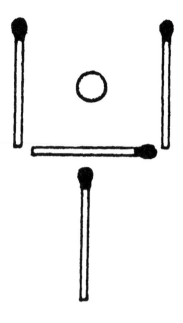

**Some solutions:** 1. Slide the horizontal match over to the right by half a match length. Pick up the upper left-hand match and put it in a vertical below the right-hand end of the horizontal match. This is usually the first solution to be arrived at. 2. Swing the two upright matches 180 degrees down. You end up with an old-fashioned glass, with a short stir stick in the middle. This solution is not often arrived at, since people usually assume that the glass has to stay in the same shape. This is a self-imposed limitation. Breakthrough solutions often come when you break away from self-imposed assumptions about the solution. 3. Pick up the two upright matches. Put the bottoms of the matches together to make a wide V. Turn the V upside down. Place it so that the base of the V is at the bottom end of the remaining lower vertical match. What you should have now is an upside down martini glass. This glass, unlike the original glass, even has a base. The solution is very rarely arrived at because it requires not only breaking through self-imposed limitations but also designing a triangular rather than a square glass shape, and therefore breaking out onto new ground.

## Form and Substance

In the cocktail glass problem, the solutions remind us of a particularly important point: Just by changing the structure and arrangement of something, we can create new things. If the glass were to be melted down, it could be reshaped to create either the old-fashioned glass or the martini glass, or a large number of other glass objects.

It is not what things are made from that gives them their essence, it is their shape and form, and the arrangement of their parts. Glasses and cups can be made from a large range of substances. We think of planes as made of aluminum, but during World War I they were made of wood and canvas, including the propellers. The idea of wooden airplanes was reborn at the end of World War II, in the form of the very high speed, twin-engined British fighter-bomber the Mosquito, which quickly became the scourge of the Luftwaffe. Keeping up with advances in wood technology, the plane was made of plywood instead of World War I–style wood frame covered by canvas.

An amusing mental game can be played with the idea of form versus substance in the case of airplanes. The DC3 passenger plane, designed before WWII and built in huge numbers during WWII, is still in operation around the world—to the tune of several thousand copies. They have been overhauled and had parts replaced so often that some have hardly any of their original pieces. Since the plane is 100 percent different in its components from the original plane, is it still the same plane? The law regards it as the same plane, it looks like the same plane. People who believe that form is everything say that it is the same plane.

This distinction between form and substance lies at the very heart of all creativity and innovation. The same eight notes can be played on the same violin, but in one arrangement and sequence they play a Mozart piece and with another a popular tune. If you remove the engine from a lawnmower and hang it on a glider, you create an ultralight airplane. In essence that's what the Wright Brothers learned how to do in 1903, with much struggle and tribulation. In the 1820s in England, there was the idea that the steam engine used for pumping water from mines could also be used to move the trolleys that ran on rails deep in the mines, except that the trolleys and rails would be put on the surface above the mine. Components that already existed were arranged to form a new combination that had theretofore not been imagined.

Every creative and innovative person I have ever met has a driving curiosity. People who lack it are rarely if ever innovative and creative, naturally have little interest in what creativity is and how it works. They ignore the question as academic and get on with a life of taking things as they are and accepting reality without trying to reinvent it. But as you move yourself from low or medium interest in innovation to higher interest and higher action, you become increasingly curious about what it is all about and how innovation happens.

That creativity consists in nothing more than putting things into new arrangements and patterns, and thereby causing something new to exist, cannot possibly be overestimated. It is also magical, because something new pops into the universe and has a sound, look, character, and function with no precedent. And it is mysterious, because there is no explanation for the fact that something genuinely new, genuinely novel, can come into being when the only thing that has taken place is a rearrangement of already existing elements and components.

Take water. At one point in the history of the universe only hydrogen existed: an electron, a proton, and a neutron. Later oxygen appeared, consisting of exactly the same components except a larger number and arranged in a different pattern. Oxygen and hydrogen are the same in composition but different in character. We breathe oxygen to live; we cannot live by breathing hydrogen. Whenever hydrogen and oxygen come together, a violent explosion occurs and a mating takes place. Out of the mating comes a product: water. Water contains only hydrogen and oxygen, but has unique properties and characteristics. You can drink water, wash with it, grow plants with it, freeze it and skate on it, and dissolve sugar and salt in it. You cannot live without it. Water constitutes over 70 percent of your body and 70 percent of the earth's surface. That hydrogen and oxygen produce water when they join together is magic. Why its properties are more than and different from either of its components is a mystery never yet explained by science.

Add an innocuous yellow element called sulfur to the water in such a way as to cause the water and the sulfur to synthesize, and still another magical and mysterious substance pops into existence: sulfuric acid, a substance so powerful that it can eat its way through steel. A piece of child's doggerel captures the fullness of the transformation:

> *Alas, poor Willie.*
> *Willie is no more,*
> *For what he thought*
> *Was H$_2$O*
> *Was H$_2$SO$_4$*

The tendency that many things have to join together and form new unions, whether physical, biological, social, or financial, is called *syntropy*, or, sometimes much more awkward, *negentropy. Entropy* is the process of things wearing down, falling apart, decaying, drifting into disorder. The maintenance, repair, and cleaning department of a manufacturing plant or office building is set up to fight entropy. On the other hand, the product design or redesign group, or the office systems and procedures group, is set up to play the syntropy game. Thus, creative breakthroughs are made by putting what already exists into new shapes and combinations. This idea forms the basis for several virtually foolproof techniques that can be used to produce new ideas, inventions, and innovations. These techniques are explained in the next chapter. But for now, let's return to our discussion of imagination, one of the brain's advanced cognitive processes.

## The Dreams of the Night

In my creativity workshops, participants have told me of how an important creative idea came to them in a dream. Usually the idea solved a problem they had been brooding over for a while. Why do ideas come to us during dreams when they haven't during the day, when we are alert and conscious? The answer is easy. Our imaginations are at their most active during dreams, and it is from the imagination that ideas come. The most fantastic, bizarre, and entertaining things go on in our dreams. Amorous adventures take place in dreams. Imaginary business meetings occur.

One of my workshop participants reported the following experience.

> Some years ago, when I was attending University, I had a thesis to write that consisted of designing a dryer with airflow, temperature, and humidity control. None of the things I read about in the journals really fit the bill. I read quite a few other publications and thought and thought about it. Finally I was at my wit's end to decide just how I would design such a device.
>
> One evening, after thinking about the problem— and I had been thinking about it for quite a few weeks— I went to bed. Oddly enough, the solution came to me in a dream. I got up and wrote it down, and had a very great sense of satisfaction in coming up with a solution so quickly.
>
> When I got up the next morning I perfected it a bit, thought about it from a practical sense, and it still seemed to fit the bill. The thesis was written. About two years later the device was actually fabricated.

Some people remember a lot of their dreams, others very few. Nonetheless, sleep research has proved that everyone has fifteen or so minutes of dreaming during their sleep at regular intervals of approximately ninety minutes. Of course, not all dreams are about practical problems related to school, work, or business. Many are trivial reenactments in disguised—yet recognizable—form of life's little problems, frustrations, wishes, enmities, or lusts. In dreams you do things that your sense of propriety, self-esteem, or morality would not permit you to do in real life, and you have feelings that are several times more intense than any you experience in daytime.

Many feelings and impulses show themselves in dreams because they are suppressed during waking hours. In dreams our instincts and thoughts are liberated from constraints. Ideas race through the brain without a need to reject or judge them. In fact, the more absurd, fantastic, or silly the ideas may be, the more entertaining or intriguing they are to the dreamer. You do not criticize yourself nor your thoughts, images, and feelings; anything goes.

When dreams do happen to be about practical problems, that

freedom of thought and imagination is invaluable because it permits a breakthrough that would never take place in the cold light of day. Let's look at some of the stories that are legendary in the history and lore of dreaming.

• *Kekule:* An early classic about a breakthrough idea that came during a dream is the story of the nineteenth-century chemist Friedrich Kekule. The scientist was in the habit of dozing in front of his fireplace during the day in the hope of getting ideas during his dreams. His work took place at the dawn of organic chemistry, when one of the questions of the day was how the carbon atoms that made up benzene were joined together. His insight came to him while he was dozing away, and here is how he described his experience:

> I turned my chair to the fire and dozed. Again the atoms were gamboling before my eyes. This time the smaller groups kept modestly in the background. My mental eye, rendered more acute by repeated visions of this kind, could now distinguish large structures of manifold conformation; long rows, sometimes more closely fitted together; all twining and twisting in snakelike motion. But look! What was that? One of the snakes had seized hold of its own tail and the form whirled mockingly before my eyes. As if by a flash of lightning, I awoke.

The image of a snake swallowing its own tail is traced to early civilizations of the East. Kekule knew the image, but it took the power of his sleeping mind to do what his waking mind could not do and use it as a clue to the ringlike structure of benzene.

Kekule went on to explain that when asked to address a large meeting of chemists on the method he used to make his discovery, he described how it had been made during a dream, not quite what the scholars had expected. But Kekule concluded his presentation by saying, "But, honored scholars, what I really learned was that in science it is important to dream."

• *Watt:* The Scottish inventor James Watt had been trying to invent a new, less expensive way of making lead shot. During a dream, he had an image of rain turning into round balls of hail. When he woke up, he immediately knew he had an answer. He constructed a high, hollow tower with a screen covering the top. Molten lead was poured in sheets across the screen, and fell like rain. By the time the rain of lead hit the ground, the soft drops had hardened into round balls of lead shot.

• *Stevenson:* The writer Robert Louis Stevenson claimed in his autobiography that everything he ever wrote had been produced in dreams, which he made happen every night by deliberate instruction to himself. He dreamed his novels chapter by chapter, night after night, and used the days to record what he had dreamed the night before. When the dream did not produce results that satisfied him, he redreamed the topic to get it right. He used deliberate dreaming not only to produce his works of fiction but also to get ideas for his many critical essays on the subject of literature. The next time you hear a reference to *Kidnapped, Treasure Island,* or any of his other works, remember how he dreamt them up.

When dreams have deep personal significance, they can be difficult to interpret. But what most of our dreams mean is often self-evident, or requires just a few minutes to puzzle out. Some people have found that they can easily make themselves dream about whatever they want. How to do deliberate dreaming is described in Chapter 9.

## Daydreaming

There is a state of consciousness you pass through at night on your way to sleep and pass through again in the morning as you wake (unless awakened abruptly) that neuroscientists call the *theta state*. It's generally described by us nonscientists as a state of being "half asleep." While you are in this state, images of the same type as appear in your dreams float across your mind. You drift in and out of theta if you doze off while watching TV or are on a long air flight and similar occasions.

Frank Ogden, a Vancouver creativity consultant and futurist, uses his morning theta state as an opportunity to do some creative thinking. When he wakes, instead of getting up immediately he allows himself to drift into theta with the intention of dreaming about his clients and their problems.

On one occasion, Ogden dreamed he was a cowboy on a horse, yet armed with the lance that medieval knights carried. He saw himself charging automobiles in his client's parking lot, piercing the bodies of employees' cars as if they were dragons. The parking lot was at the foot of the client's ski hill, and every employee car meant one less customer could use the hill. That dream led to a discussion with the client about a parking area for employees, where cars could be arranged a distance away, with a shuttle to and from it. The solution freed up a significant number of parking spaces for customers. As is the case so often with breakthrough ideas, this solution seemed obvious after the fact, yet the answer was not forthcoming until a dream produced it.

Here's another case: During a long and varied career as CEO of such companies and organizations as Alcan, Nabisco Brands, and Tambrands, Martin Emmett used to daydream in the evenings in a deliberate way. He found that these daydreams helped him come up with unexpected solutions to particularly obdurate problems. The method was to sit in an easy chair after dinner, put on some earphones, and listen to pleasant music while he drifted into a relaxed state of mind. The dreams and images floated by, presenting him with often bizarre ideas but also occasionally with practical and unexpected breakthroughs. This method of dreaming up ideas was something he stumbled across himself. Now that the method has been scientifically validated, he can, without apology or embarrassment, advocate it for general use.

## Simulating the Dream State

Moral and practical judgment is cut off from its normal operation while we are asleep and dreaming. We are in a primitive state of mind. Imagination and fantasy run wild. Emotions are activated in an intensity that exceeds anything we feel during the day. Could we get at least slightly into that state of mind during the day, other than with hard drugs? Yes. If we could reduce our inhibitions and turn off our judgment, could we cause ourselves to come up with breakthrough ideas? Again, yes.

There are several ways to get closer to the dream state while still awake. I encountered the first way thirty-five years ago, with a method developed by Alex Osborn, an advertising executive. Developed originally for group use, Osborn's method focused on turning off judgment and inhibitions while encouraging an outpouring of uncensored thoughts. The idea was not new, having been in use by artists and poets for centuries, but Osborn made it work in a business setting. Probably the most popular and widely used idea-generating method ever, he called it brainstorming. Osborn emphasized that the attempt was to produce the most ideas possible, with no attempt at quality. The concept of quality is judgmental, and judgment was to be used only later, when the ideas generated by the brainstorming would be examined, evaluated, and then developed as appropriate. During these idea-generating sessions, the rule was that no criticism be made and no discussion or analysis take place until all ideas were presented.

The extraordinary generative power of suspended judgment became clear to me a long time ago, when I used it with Dyeco, a small specialty chemical company in Kingston, Ontario. I was teaching at that time at Queen's University School of Business. Dan Atack, the young company president and a chemical engineer by profession, phoned me one day, introduced himself, and announced that his company was stagnant and performing poorly. If something significant were not done, the company was certainly going to wither away. They'd tried everything, he explained, but nothing was giving them any revitalization. They needed some new ideas. Dr. Atack, the founder of the company, had died; Dan, his brother Jim—a business graduate and accountant—and a third member of the management, a chemist, now owned controlling interest. Both Dan and Jim were active in community affairs; Dan was president of the city's Young Men's Christian Association and Jim of the Children's Aid Society.

I suggested they try brainstorming. Might as well, he replied. I also told him that, while I had never used it, it sounded simple to do. We subsequently had a twenty-minute session, in which Dan,

Jim, and three or four others participated. I acted as facilitator. All of us were astonished at how fast the ideas flew. In the end, we had produced some sixty thoughts, some of them salacious, others inane, and none seeming to make sense. The mood got quite silly during the session, as each absurd idea poured forth, along with a few that were prosaic and matter-of-fact. At one point, Jim yelled, "Fire the guards." Under normal circumstances, such an idea would never have been thought, never mind expressed, so strong was the group's sense of responsibility for the employees. It was also one that made no sense for a chemical company, with dangerous materials in storage that obviously had to be watched twenty-four hours a day, seven days a week. Certainly we had succeeded in suspending judgment, but where was the quality?

The Osborn method called for an evaluation session to be held at a later time. The session was to examine all the ideas produced in the brainstorming session, looking for possible gems in everything that had been said. In the evaluation session the next day, an incredible thing happened: The thought "Fire the guards," which had seemed improper, was the answer. Dyeco's plant was a small structure that stood alone, in the middle of a large field. The stationary engineers, who were on duty twenty-four hours a day to produce the steam needed for heating and processing, made regular rounds as watchmen. It was decided that instead of having the plant watched by these human guards, it could be protected by a high fence and an alarm system tied into police and fire headquarters. The company's stationary engineers could then be replaced by automated equipment running on natural gas. The idea of a chemical plant standing sixteen hours a day in an empty field without watchmen on the premises initially seemed absurd and foolhardy. In fact, it took quite a few minutes of discussion and reflection before the idea began to take on a measure of plausibility. Ultimately it was implemented, and the resulting reduction in overhead was impressive. Dan had no difficult finding other jobs for the employees with other companies in the town.

"Through these and other actions," Jim told me, "we were able to lower the break-even point of the company by 40 percent. Although we had started this overhead reduction process before you came, using systematic analysis, the big gains came after your session through the use of creative thinking to challenge 'sacred assumptions.' " The event thus began a new era in which reliance was placed on doing innovative and creative thinking all the time. It is thirty five years later and the owners are comfortably retired. When the company was sold, the price per share gave them almost a hundred to one on the amount they had originally paid for the shares.

The single experience with suspended judgment and unconstrained imagination made an indelible impression on the minds of all involved. The first attempts to break out of the bind they were in had been the usual logical analysis of facts and figures and examination of business alternatives. But twenty minutes of acting like uninhibited children had done what reason and judgment could not. Keeping an open mind, letting the mind wander, exploring a wide range of possibilities, and being less judgmental are essential to making breakthroughs and creating innovative solutions.

Jim, the business major, later complained that the way the solution was obtained ran absolutely contrary to everything he had been taught in business school. Facts, logic, hard-nosed analysis, common sense, sound judgment, and hard work was the business formula that he had been programmed to believe in and work by. Now a new business formula had made its presence known, an antiformula that set each of his beliefs on its head. But eventually the shock was absorbed and digested. The realization set in that in business, both ways of thinking and acting were valid. One was for making breakthroughs, inventions, and innovations, and the other was for implementing them and for doing routine things in conventional ways. Jim eventually went back to university, took a doctorate in sociology, and became an internal management consultant for the federal government. Retired early from government employment, he now teaches creative approaches to changing organizations and government programs at Queen's University.

The story also contains a profound irony. When I first met him, Jim's hobbies were poetry and painting, even while he, being a business major, was the one who handled the firm's finances and accounting procedures. He pointed out to me recently that although he had been thoroughly into creative processes in his poetry and painting, at the time our story unfolded, these creative processes were to him "hobbies, not tools for running a business."

## THE FUN SIDE OF CREATIVITY

It is next to impossible to be creative without being amused sometime during the creative process. In creativity workshops, people laugh out loud or smile with delight whenever they come up with insightful answers. Having an insight is like hearing the punch line to a good joke. Both produce an adrenal surge, a rush of delight. Both fulfill our need as humans to experience physical and emotional sensations and give us joy in being alive. Creativity and innovation provide the same excitement as people get from games and puzzles. You never know whether you'll win or lose, or whether there will be tears or laughter. In the beginning there is challenge and frustration; at the end, there is pleasure and triumph or dismay and disappointment. Creativity blurs the distinction between work and play—it makes work fun and fun makes money.

I recall vividly the resistance an executive in a creative thinking workshop had to suspending judgment. He folded his arms and proclaimed that there was no way he was going to act like a fool. He took himself too seriously. He kept his mouth shut while the rest of his group went wild with erratic thoughts. He wanted a way of producing ideas while keeping his feet on the ground. He'll still be looking. And I've found that many people are like him. They are admirable people, but they never have a new idea. Nursing a false sense of pride and dignity, they never joke or act spontaneously.

Times have changed, but our need for laughter hasn't. Nor has the need to poke holes in preposterous notions put forth with somber seriousness in management circles. The courts of old used to have jesters, whose function was to poke fun at the nobles, including the king. Jesters were encouraged to say outrageous things—half in jest and half to expose unexamined beliefs and habits and let in fresh air and thought. Putting cartoons like *Dilbert* on bulletin boards is not a bad start. "Thank God It's Friday" parties are another good idea. These create an atmosphere of fun and irreverence. Think up a few ideas for how you can inject more levity into your group meetings.

1. _____

2. _____

3. _____

Creativity is a field full of anomalies and ironies. Take, for example, the question of originality. The truth is that many celebrated breakthroughs and innovations are nothing more than legal steals. One is a theft from nature, the other a theft from a domain different from the one you're working in.

## Bio-Mimicry

Thefts from nature are common: dams from beavers, nets from spiders, traps from carnivorous flowers, poison darts from bees, airplane wings from birds, tanks from turtles, camouflage from chameleons, pliers from lobsters. The fancy term for this thievery is *bio-mimicry*, and I discuss it at greater length in Chapter 9. One of its more recent examples is Velcro, an invention made when the burrs on a dog's fur were examined under microscope and their hooking mechanism copied. Another example is the landing gear on one of the U.S. Navy's carrier planes, which mimics the legs of a grasshopper.

## Concept Displacement

When an idea that worked in one field is applied in another field, this form of theft goes by the name of *concept displacement*. For example, a surgeon at the Royal Victoria Hospital in Montreal got the bright idea of sewing a large zipper over the incisions of abdominal patients who had to have their wounds periodically opened so as to drain internal cavities. This technique has saved hundreds of lives and is now used worldwide. The doctor got the idea when he was out jogging and saw a long zipper on the vest of a tailor's dummy as he passed by a display window. It took a remarkable leap of imagination to see that zippers could be used to open and close living flesh, not only cloth.

Another example is the way acting has been applied in fields such as psychotherapy and training. In socio-drama, a method of psychotherapy developed by psychologist Moreno, a man and wife (for example) act out some typical argument or conflict in the presence of a therapist. The scene, when videotaped, can later be analyzed and discussed by the couple with the aid of the therapist. In sales training, one trainee attempts a presentation of the product to another, while the trainer and the rest of the class deal with other matters. The scene is videotaped and then analyzed, with everyone learning from the mistakes and successes that occurred during the scene.

## Summing Up

Although there is still more not known about the creativity process than there is known, what we do know is useful for a business setting. We know, for example, how to increase our success rate at making breakthroughs and produce more innovative ideas. As humans we are endowed with brains designed to produce ideas, and we can deliberately learn to be more creative. If you have a talent for writing, you can become a more creative writer. If your talent is salesmanship, you can come up with creative ways to relate to your clients. Whatever your talent, you can employ it creatively and obtain greater satisfaction.

Creative thinking is both similar to and different from everyday thinking. Creative thinking has less respect for simple logic, ordinary facts, and common sense, and draws heavily on our powers of perception, intuition, and imagination. The unconscious parts of our minds are where new ideas are often born. Recognizing this, we can do many things to make its work easier. Many breakthroughs have been born in dreams or are produced by accident. We know that a key to discovery is always looking at things from different angles and new viewpoints. Exploration and divergent thinking are crucial to discovery and invention. Ideas flow more freely when we release ourselves from the constraints of judgment and criticism, and let our impulses have free rein.

Even getting ideas while asleep represents a way of using the human mind that is the opposite of that which we have been taught. Diverging and converging are two opposing processes. Brainstorming is the opposite of behavior in polite company. And so it goes. Plainly, opposites have a lot to do with creative thinking, in respect to the kinds of results that are produced and the processes that produce them.

Creative thinking is a process in which you switch back and forth between opposite moods, mental processes, and actions. By so doing, you can direct your creative energies with mastery and purpose. The switches include:

- Actively searching for information and knowledge, and passive relaxation to allow it to assimilate
- Moving about in the outdoors, and holing up in an office or den
- Getting passionately involved with a project, and enjoying quiet contemplation of it
- Studying hard, undeniable facts, and exploring questionable speculations and fantasies
- Thinking of colorful images and imaginative metaphors, and using precise numbers and exact words
- Spending time in introverted, solitary thinking about your challenges, and being in gregarious interactions and dialogue about it with colleagues and friends
- Actively experimenting on your project, and doing purely mental things on paper

# Chapter 9

# AUXILIARY THINKING TOOLS

"Most new ideas are discovered by perceiving the relationship or analogy between two quite different fields of activity."

—Arthur Koestler

While it's clear that creativity and innovation have their adventurous side, there are also some practical aspects. Like a wily hunter, the innovator employs a variety of tools, tactics, and techniques to track down his elusive prey. These methods can have great power, consequently it's interesting to examine some of them.

In this chapter, I look at six common thinking tools. No one uses all six—usually it's a favorite one or two. But each is described in enough detail that you will have little trouble putting it to work for you.

## TIME AND PLACE

Ideas prefer to make their appearance at certain times and in certain places; conversely, other times and places aren't so good. One place people tell me they rarely get ideas is at work and when they're working. Or when they do get ideas at work, it's during a coffee break or gathered around the proverbial water cooler.

Give some thought to where and when your best ideas come. I've listed below various times and places where people tell me they have had most ideas come to them. In the blank spaces I've provided, write the words *often, seldom,* or *never.* Doing this exercise will remind you to take advantage of these best times and places, and perhaps to find some others that you've been neglecting.

| | |
|---|---|
| in bed | _____ |
| in the shower | _____ |
| when jogging | _____ |
| in a swimming pool | _____ |
| in a fishing boat | _____ |
| in the car | _____ |
| over lunch | _____ |
| when gardening | _____ |
| around the house at night or during the weekend | _____ |
| in a hotel room | _____ |
| in an airplane | _____ |
| when painting a fence, cutting grass, or raking leaves | _____ |

Ron Holmes, an engineering manager at Honeywell in Freeport, Illinois, happened to own a small hobby farm situated on the bank of a river just three miles from the plant. He and his team would sometimes head to the farmhouse at noontime to eat a picnic lunch on the verandah and watch the river flow lazily by. They'd eat, look, and relax, and chat about the situations and opportunities facing them back at the plant. They'd often come up with excellent ideas. Not surprisingly, these noontime picnics became a regular habit—pleasant, relaxing, and profitable all at once.

You probably don't have a farmhouse on a river near your office, but there are other places you might find. For example, how about a nearby hotel suite that can be rented occasionally for a two-hour, easygoing think-in with a picnic-style lunch of sandwiches and coffee? Martin Emmett, the CEO of a large division of Alcan, wrestled a long-standing profitability problem to the ground with a breakthrough idea that came out of one such free-floating bull session in a hotel suite just around the corner from the corporate office. Earlier attempts to solve the problem during formal shoulder-to-the-wheel meetings in company conference rooms had gotten nowhere. But tackling the problem in a relaxed setting turned out to be absolutely correct.

A department store executive rented a boat for a two-hour luncheon cruise around Toronto harbor for a dozen people from his shoe department. The purpose was to come up with new ideas for the Christmas season, and all kinds of good ideas spilled out. Christmas sales that year hit an unprecedented peak.

There are always the ways and means to find better places and times for idea generation. Before going any further, write down three that you can come up with right now.

1. _____
2. _____
3. _____

Even the office can be turned into a place where it's OK to stop work and just trade ideas. Most companies have a no-nonsense atmosphere—nose to the grindstone and tail in the air, all day long. Chewing the fat or aimless conversation is not tolerated, never mind desired. But does it have to be that way? Can a looser atmosphere be created? You could gain some special advantages that might pay off in bigger rewards.

In one of my seminars in England, a participant described his unusual creative experience at Hawker-Siddeley, an aircraft manufacturing company. He and his group were jawing over things at the end of a particularly long day's work. The conversation drifted to one of their chronic exasperations: adding items to the computer production of a twenty-seven-volume illustrated parts catalogue for the Trident airplane. When a new item had to be added, it was no problem providing there was space available on the page. If not, all remaining pages had to be redesigned and renumbered, requiring a huge computer time load; there could be as many as 2,000 pages in a single volume. Because of the frequent additions, every volume had to be reprinted two or three times a year.

As they got talking, one man dreamed of a page that could be folded like an accordion. Another yearned for rubber paper that could be stretched when new information had to be squeezed in. The group's mood got zanier, perhaps owing to the fatigue of an eleven-hour day. But suddenly the tired minds snapped and out popped an unexpected solution! Number the pages 30A, 30B, 30C, etc. Next, design a computer program that could automatically renumber whenever a new catalogue item got created. The group was elated. Hawker-Siddeley was also able to license this new computer cataloguing system to a number of competing aviation companies.

The experience had an enormous effect on the group's propensity to look for novel ideas. And individuals became more likely to toss loony ideas into their discussions anytime the impulse hit them. To boot, they all became more open to the ideas of others.

Some companies have developed deliberate strategies for making the workplace an ideal spot for generating breakthrough ideas. Research has shown that the most creative R&D engineers are often the ones who do the most talking and chatting with their peers and have little hesitation sharing ideas. As a result, some companies have designed the rooms and walkways of engineering buildings so as to encourage conversation. For example, chairs, chalkboards, and easels are set up where people are most likely to bump into each other and start a conversation.

Other companies take a different tack, and create special think-tank rooms. General Foods in Toronto was one such company. It leapt at the idea the moment it was brought up in a creative thinking and innovation workshop. GF called the room the Idea Center, and it had floor-to-ceiling windows overlooking a wooded, hilly parkland. People's eyes were drawn outward from the room to the hills and trees and to the sky. It was exactly the kind of view that Peter Curzon, the General Foods staff executive who set up the room, wanted it to have.

The equipment and decor were chosen with equal attention to their effect on employees' creative thought processes. The furnishings are those you would find in a home rather than an office: soft, deep chairs, low coffee tables, and sculptures. Large house plants and wood sculptures of animals caused the room to seem to be both inside and outside at the same time. Then, to suggest that bizarre or strange ideas might not be out of place, there were a couple of surrealistic prints on the walls. An oversized carved wooden pear, easily two feet in diameter, was placed on a coffee table. Meetings in the Idea Center went on nonstop, as one group after the other used it and ideas poured forth. The Idea Center proved to be one of the most cost-effective actions the company had ever taken.

# THE BACK BURNER

The back-burner technique assumes that the project you are working on is not one where you are likely to get a quick answer, and you are prepared for the long haul. Here are the things you do.

1. *Collect information on the subject.* Go to the library. Read books, periodicals, magazines, listen to tapes, watch videos. Visit and talk to people. Ask them lots of questions, and keep notes on index cards, in a notebook, or on a pocket dictating machine.

2. *Keep reviewing your notes.* Think about your project every time you can. Tell people about it, and ask them for their ideas. Listen with an open mind. The slightest thing they say may trigger an association that turns out to be helpful.

3. *Put the project on the back burner from time to time.* Forget about it for a day or two, or even a week. Take a short holiday. Work on some completely different project. Let the project incubate. Even though you are unaware of it, your mind will keep at it, with no conscious attention on your part.

4. *Write down ideas as they come to you.* Put each idea on a separate card. Lay out the cards on a table and arrange them into groups or classes. See what connections you can find among the ideas.

5. *Be persistent.* Either bit by bit or all at once, the insights will come. The way you see the problem will keep changing, getting clearer. Keep the faith; it almost certainly will work out. If you keep your brain working with periodic inputs and efforts, waking or sleeping, you will get the answer.

## ALPHA AND THETA REVERIE

There is a method for getting your mind into either of two states, called alpha and theta reverie, respectively. These states are excellent for doing the loose, associative thinking conducive to freeing ideas from the unconscious. But before I describe the method, it is best to look exactly at what these two states of consciousness, called alpha and theta, are like.

Reflect on the fact that from time to time everyone, including yourself, lets his or her mind wander away from the work at hand. You daydream a bit about other, often more personal, things. After a moment or two, you catch yourself, feel momentarily embarrassed, and turn your thoughts back to the work you were doing.

If you spend a lot of time daydreaming, particularly about goals and perspectives, you are behaving the way high achievers behave. Researchers have found that high achievers do much more daydreaming than do nonachievers. High achievers engage in what researchers call *chronic fantasizing*. To illustrate, one entrepreneur—the successful owner of three small newspapers—calls what she does "dreamin' and schemin'."

In their fantasizing, entrepreneurs and innovators often come up with their most profitable ideas. On the other hand, people who daydream very little, who keep their eyes relentlessly focused on the task at hand, are low- or medium-level achievers. Ironically, these underachievers often have more talent and ability than high achievers do, but high achievers have greater dreams, and they spend more time dreaming about how to fulfill them. Let's look a little more deeply, then, into the serious business of daydreaming.

Everyone knows that we spend our lives in one of two basic states, awake and asleep, which we alternate between endlessly from birth to death. But not everyone knows that being awake takes the form of one of three states, called beta, alpha, and theta.

In the beta state, you are alert and focused, and your attention is on doing something—say, talking on the phone or writing a letter. If electrodes were attached to your head while you were in this beta state and connected to an oscilloscope, the waves on the monitor would show a fairly rapid frequency of 13 to 19 oscillations per second, technically referred to as 13 to 19 Hertz (Hz).

At other times you are in a more relaxed state of mind called alpha, and the frequency is 6 to 13 Hz, showing a shallower, slower pattern than beta. This would likely be your state of mind if you were in a park on a nice June day, wandering around a bit and sitting on a bench in the warm glow of the sun. You are calm and serene, very relaxed.

## Alpha Relaxation

During alpha state, your thoughts are not focused but wander aimlessly from one topic to another in a loose flow of free association. This is a good time to daydream about that new plant you are thinking of building or that better organizational arrangement you have been pondering. New ideas and deeper insights are more likely to come now than ever would be the case during beta state.

The following fifteen-minute procedure describes how easily you can get yourself into an alpha state. Having done so, you will be able to spend another fifteen minutes free-associating and maybe come up with a creative solution to whatever challenge you have chosen to work on.

1. Find yourself a dimly lit, quiet room and a straight-backed chair to sit on.

2. Sit on the chair, relaxed but squarely upright, not slouched. Place your hands on your thighs, palms down, lightly and comfortably.

3. Silently and slowly repeat the sound "om" for a few moments, perhaps ten or twenty times.

4. Let the sound slowly soften as you say it and gradually let it become softer and softer until it seems to disappear. Your mind, you find, is now completely blank.

5. Let your mind stay blank for a while. You'll find, however, that thoughts start wandering up to the surface from somewhere or other, drifting across your mind almost like bubbles.

6. Watch these thoughts float by, one by one, but don't interfere with them. Just let them be and observe them quietly for a while.

7. After a short bit, go back again to repeating the sound "om" and repeat the cycle. Keep cycling through the sequence, easily and effortlessly, for a total of about twenty minutes. At the end, count slowly up to 10 and open your eyes.

During the fifteen minutes, you will be surprised to find that your thoughts are only loosely connected and tend to be of a trivial nature. They seem to come from nowhere, drift slowly across your consciousness, and then disappear from view. In the brief period after you let the sound of "om" gradually subside, you find your mind strangely empty of thoughts. This is sometimes referred to as *contentless consciousness* and it contrasts starkly with our normal waking consciousness. To find your mind momentarily empty of all thought is a surprising experience.

After you open your eyes, you will be pleased to see how relaxed you feel, how calm you are, how light your body feels. You'll also notice how clear your mind is, as if cobwebs had been swept away from in front of it. Now you are ready for some serious but easygoing associative thinking about your project. It's an opportunity for some associative mental exploration. Just remember, of course, that you are hunting not for just any ideas but for ideas of a paradoxical nature.

## Theta Consciousness

Theta is the state that you are momentarily in when you drift into sleep at night, and again when you come out of sleep in the morning. During theta, you feel half awake and half asleep. As in alpha, you are relaxed and calm, even blissful. But there is one remarkable difference: In theta, images and not just thoughts wander through your mind, just as they do in the dreams you have at night. In this sense, theta is true dreaming. Your brain wave frequency is 5 to 8 Hz—even slower than during alpha. Theta is an excellent state of mind for creative thinking.

Getting into theta state is exactly the same for alpha, except that you keep the process going longer, until you find images drifting across your mind rather than thoughts. The images usually involve activity and can have almost any content imaginable.

I still remember the first time I succeeded in deliberately getting into theta, which had taken me several attempts. The first image that came across my mind was that of a motorcyclist turning a bend on a narrow mountain road. I still don't know what the image represented or why it came to me from seemingly nowhere. But I learned in a subsequent theta session that I could evoke visual images of whatever I wanted.

It's not difficult to get images floating up in your mind. You can see them in detail, even color. And you can manipulate these images as well. Using theta, an engineer can conjure up the picture of a machine or a tool. A salesperson can create a picture of a sales call and mentally try out several techniques.

## DELIBERATE DREAMING

As you go to sleep, you pass from a theta state into a state of light sleep known as Rapid Eye Movement sleep, usually referred to as REM sleep. During REM sleep, the eyes stay in constant movement for ten to twenty minutes and the brain waves show a frequency of 4 or 5 Hz. It is during this period that dreaming takes place. REM sleep is also known as Delta 1 sleep, to distinguish it from deep, or Delta 2, sleep, which has a frequency of 1 to 3 Hz and during which dreams, at least of a visual nature, are not known to occur.

It is possible, even likely, that some of our best ideas may take shape during deep sleep, and that we discover them later, either during further sleep or when we wake up. But what we want to talk about here is the dreaming that we do in Delta 1 and how to direct it to creative purposes.

Although many people say they never or rarely dream, this is not true. Researchers wake people while their eyes are moving beneath their lids and they exhibit a brain wave frequency of 4 to 5 Hz. When awakened, they always report that they have been dreaming. Every person dreams several times a night.

The time spent dreaming totals over an hour a night. That amounts to about eight hours a week—equivalent to a day's work. So people dream, and dream a lot. That some people hardly remember their dreams, that some remember many of their dreams, and that some deny that they dream at all is largely a reflection of personal habit. When you become more interested in your dreams, you will find yourself remembering more of them each morning when you wake. One of the most interesting things about dreams is that they can be made to happen.

It is possible to cause yourself to dream about almost anything you want, from holidays and work to sex and adventure, or from family matters to finance. The potential benefits of deliberate dreaming are incalculable. Imagination is at its peak during sleep, as the mind frees itself from the constraints of daytime reality. The mind, through its ability to dream, is free to entertain those things that could be, that exist in the realm of the possible and the conceivable, that can be but that have not yet come to pass. How do you deliberately dream? Here are the steps:

1. Resolve to have a dream about a project where you hope to come up with a breakthrough idea.

2. Remind yourself that the breakthrough you want should be paradoxical in character. Be sure you are in a robustly paradoxical mind-set.

3. For several days, read, think, and talk about the project and feed information and thoughts about it into your mind.

4. If you can, have a relaxing day. Perhaps play golf, or do something equally pleasant. Make yourself feel good. Think about how great it's going to feel when you come up with your breakthrough solution. Make sure your evening is pleasant, too.

5. As you drift into sleep, do so with the goal firmly in mind that this night you intend to dream about your project and that you will succeed.

6. If you wake during the night from a dream about the project, write down the answer or whatever you remember of the dream. Or dictate it into a tape recorder that you have at your bedside table.

If you get an answer, the job is done. If not, discuss whatever dream you had about the project. The answer may spring forth during the conversation. Some people have the habit of discussing their dreams with their spouses or steady companions almost every morning. It is a good habit to have, because dreams are almost always providers of some insight or awareness. In this case, even if they have not given a direct answer, they may add to your awareness of the problem.

Now that you have started your program of deliberate dreaming, go through the process again and again, night after night. The law of persistence that applies to all creativity and innovation also applies to deliberate dreaming.

## METAPHORS AND ANALOGIES

Our everyday speech is full of metaphors and analogies. We say things like, "He was caught between a rock and a hard place" instead of saying "He had to choose between two equally difficult options." A metaphor implies that one thing is similar to another. It communicates immensely because it is figurative, evoking the sensations and power of words. The image of being between a rock and a hard place says volumes about what it is like to be in a predicament where the choices are equally unpalatable. An analogy is a broader comparison, implying that if two things agree in some respects, they will probably agree in other ways as well.

Metaphors and analogies are part of our way of thinking and communicating. To persuade or explain, companies don't say, "Buy our gasoline," they say, "Put a tiger in your tank." The metaphorical phrases are endless: "Bite the bullet," "Take the market by storm," "Full speed ahead," "Bark out orders," "Strike while the iron is hot," "Make hay while the sun shines," "Water under the bridge." Here are some other commonly used similes and metaphors:

| | |
|---|---|
| An ironclad argument | Cutting out deadwood |
| Tight as a drum | Packaging the program |
| A peaches and cream complexion | Dodging issues |
| Straight as an arrow | Facing facts |
| Shaking like a leaf | Software |

Slippery as an eel                     Going down the tube
Selling like hotcakes                  Tempest in a teapot
Administrative machinery

Metaphors put the brain's power of imagery to work. If we fail to make use of metaphors in our communicating, we miss out on one of the most powerful capabilities of our brains. A metaphor is indeed worth more than a thousand words; it shakes us up, puts our mind to work, and communicates much detail and information.

Metaphors also remind us that we live in a world where things are both similar and different from each other. They help us keep the similarities in mind. Interestingly, the more creative a person is, the more likely he or she is to see the similarities between objects, between people, and between things. Think of how Isaac Newton was able to see the similarity between an apple and the moon, and to recognize their common gravitational pull toward the earth. Increasing your habit of seeing similarities will enable you to think in metaphorical ways and lead you to more insights and discoveries.

But it's not just that metaphorical images are laden with information. They have a way of penetrating the essence of things. That's why our dreams rely heavily on analogies and metaphors. You may have dreamed of being stopped by a traffic cop for speeding, only to realize later, when you were awake, that the dream was telling you that you were rushing a new product onto the market too fast and that you'd better slow down or be called to account for going too fast and courting disaster. Taken literally, that dream means nothing, but taken metaphorically it may mean that your job is at stake.

You have two ways of thinking, the metaphorical and the literal. Both are valuable, but metaphors are essential to creative thought. You hope to strike gold by ending up with a solution that entails paradox because paradoxical answers have great power. How do you use metaphors to make breakthroughs? Here's how:

1. *Formulate your goal as explicitly as you can.* Let's say the goal is to reduce costs and reduce waste.

2. *Eliminate worn-out metaphors.* There'll always be several, no matter what the objective is. One of the most common is the

"cutting" metaphor. We are going to cut costs, cut waste, cut overhead, cut payroll. It's so common and tired a metaphor that we forget it is in fact nothing but a metaphor. The same can be said of other clichés for reducing costs and expenditures, like "tightening our belts," "shrinking our budget," "tying our purse strings," "freezing expenditures." It's not that these aren't good metaphors, it's just that they've been milked dry. So recall these familiar metaphors to get them out of the way. Newer metaphors may produce newer ideas.

3. *Think up some new metaphors.* What comes to mind? Pulverizing costs (which means turning them into powder)? Annihilating costs (which means killing them)? Evaporating costs (which means boiling them)? How about "scaring them away," "sending them to Siberia," "making them wither," "sending them out to sea," "making them run for cover." These are not original metaphors, but at least their application to cost reduction is original. But how about some really original metaphors? What is a cost reduction like? Getting rid of an unwelcome visitor? Recovering from a hangover? Waking on a spring morning to find the snow all gone? Kicking off your shoes? Cleaning up a muddy creek? Vacuuming a dirty pool?

4. *Pick one of the new metaphors.* A methodology called *synectics* is one of several approaches that use metaphors and analogies. The synectics people suggest that you pick an analogy that is a little strange in the sense that it's not immediately clear that it's an analogy at all. I think "kicking off your shoes" may fit the bill.

5. *Milk the analogy for new ideas.* Will the analogy give you some new ideas? Shoes are good things because they protect us and give us support, but at a price. They're not as comfortable as the unclad foot, yet we wear them often when we don't need support or protection. We have the choice of slippers, socks, or bare feet, so why do we constrain ourselves when it serves no purpose and entails a disadvantage? We consider it ludicrous, for example, to wear street shoes while walking on a soft sand beach, as former President Nixon had the misfortune to be photographed doing. Do we not run up a lot of costs in our businesses by constraining ourselves with rules or procedures that cost a lot but serve little purpose?

For example, it's one thing to itemize when the items are each a hundred or more dollars, but it doesn't make sense to consume expensive executive and accounting time listing such small items as individual meals on a five-day trip. Why wear tight shoes all the time—how about loosening up? These ideas may not appeal to you, but your own ideas will. Try to think of other examples for reducing costs by taking off the tight shoes. They could add up to a large amount when spread wide enough.

## BIO-MIMICRY

The world is full of things that are both different from one another and similar at the same time. On one hand, even though two apples look the same, when they are viewed closely there are always differences. On the other hand, when such different-looking things as oranges and bananas are examined for similarities, lots are to be found: both are edible, both are fruit, both have skins, both are tasty, both are grown in warm climates, both have seeds. Both apples and oranges, like other objects of nature, are similar to manufactured objects such as baseballs, croquet balls, and crystal balls. In fact, it's easy to speculate that before the first men or women invented a ball for their kids to toss about, possibly made of cloth or leather, the kids had probably been using apples, small coconuts, or something similar in their games. Man-made balls are a direct steal from nature.

There is good reason to believe that many early inventions were made by observing something in nature and then making a copy. Be that as it may, what is certain is that an increasing number of modern inventions are the result of human efforts to copy nature. The classic example, mentioned earlier, is Velcro, invented in 1948. Velcro's inventor, inspired by the tenacity with which burrs stuck to his socks, examined a few of them under a microscope. What he saw was that burrs had hundreds of tiny hooked barbs which enabled them to cling so successfully and obstinately to his socks. The next step for the inventor was to find a way to create a human equivalent. Nylon filament is the material most often used to weave Velcro. It takes about twelve pounds of force per square inch to separate two pieces of Velcro.

If you are looking for paradoxical inventions in nature, they are not hard to find. Examples of paradoxes in nature (or what appear to be paradoxes) are:

Flying squirrels
Flying fish
Birds that can't fly, such as ostriches and penguins
Whales, which live in the water yet are mammals and breathe air
Tropical plants that trap and eat mice and lizards
Trees that, instead of breathing in oxygen and exhaling $CO_2$ as animals do, breathe in $CO_2$ and exhale oxygen
Rosebushes, whose colorful flowers attract insects but whose thorns repulse animals

None of the above may have any relevance to your project. They are meant just as demonstrations of the extent to which paradoxical situations can be found in nature. Try generating a list of examples of your own.

Bio-mimicry is in constant use as a tool for discovery and invention. When it first came to be recognized as an important research method, it was called *bionics*, but that usage was abandoned when the word came into general use as a term for equipping humans with artificial limbs and organs.

So to find paradoxical solutions in nature, search out organisms, plants, animals, birds, or fish that have characteristics you want to copy, using man-made materials and devices.

## SUMMARY

A variety of powerful auxiliary methods are available to help you in your quest for paradoxical answers. They are all methods that allow you to activate certain basic mental processes so as to have fresh mental associations, new links to form between ideas, and breakthrough insights and ideas. Using at least one or two of these methods is a virtual necessity. In any case, their frequent employment promises that your creativity and innovation will reach levels they have never reached before. Keep in mind that it will be your own imagination and ingenuity that will produce the answers—by themselves the auxiliary methods do nothing. It is only your own determination and tenacity—normal attributes you were born with—that can make such methods useful.

# Chapter 10

# SOME FUN: MIND TRAINING EXERCISES

"Man's mind stretched to a new idea never goes back to its original dimension."

—Oliver Wendell Holmes

You can develop your mind to do a variety of tasks better. For example, if you wanted to use more metaphors in your writing, you could do it by repetition and practice. It might take quite a while, but eventually the metaphor habit would be ingrained in your behavior. When you practice mental skills, you lay down new neural pathways in your brain. Practice makes perfect, it's said. Constant practice of mental skills may not turn your brain into a perfect thinking machine, but it will make it work better.

The exercises in this chapter will sharpen your ability to recognize, visualize, and creatively manipulate opposites. Some of them have to do with ideas, some with stories, some with letters and words, some with numbers, and some with pictures. If you run through them hurriedly, they won't do much except maybe provide you with a bit of fun. You can only train your brain if you go slowly, put energy and concentration into each item, and reflect on what you are doing.

Optimally, you should do these exercises in a group led by a facilitator who can keep the pace just right and makes sure the concentration is maintained. But in lieu of that, you must apply the discipline yourself. There are easily enough exercises here for a full day's work and discussion, if not a lot more.

# THE SAYINGS

All through history people have used opposites to express their opinions.

You'll find some of the following sayings to be straightforward, ironic, or satirical—and others enigmatic. Some are silly and others are serious. But in every case, they can sharpen your sense of the ironic and enhance your ability to use paradox as the springboard for insights and discoveries.

Read the following quotations, then rate them on a scale from 1 to 5 in terms of meaning for you. Be prepared to explain to your partner or your group why the saying has such value.

1. *Out of life comes death and out of death life, out of the young the old, out of waking sleep, the stream of creation and dissolution never stops.*
   —Heraclitus                                  _____

2. *Much more would be done if people believed less was impossible.*
   —Francois de Malherbes                       _____

3. *Forty is the old age of youth; fifty, the youth of old age.*
   —Goethe                                      _____

4. *In strategy it is important to see distant things as if they were close and to take a distanced view of close things.*
   —Myamoto Masabi                              _____

5. *Our language has wisely sensed the two sides of being alone. It has created the word loneliness to express the pain of being alone. And it has created the word solitude to express the glory of being alone.*
   —Paul Tillich                                _____

6. *The difference between perseverance and obstinacy is that one often comes from a strong will, and the other from a strong won't.*
   —Beechen                                              _____

7. *Art is a lie that makes us realize truth.*
   —Pablo Picasso                                        _____

8. *Most men know what they hate, few know what they love.*
   —Anonymous                                            _____

9. *We have to be careful not to lock ourselves into one side of a situation or another not recognizing that underlying it all there is only one essential thing and that in that unity all opposites support each other.*
   —Swami Chetanananda                                   _____

10. *The paradox is the source of the thinker's passion, and the thinker without a paradox is like a lover without feeling, a paltry mediocrity.*
    —Anonymous                                           _____

11. *Nothing is so firmly believed as that which is not known.*
    —Jean Jacques Rousseau                               _____

12. *If there were no bad people, there would be no good lawyers.*
    —Charles Dickens                                     _____

13. *It is a strange world of language in which skating on thin ice can get you into hot water.*
    —Franklin P. Jones                                   _____

14. *The bad thing about good things is that they come to an end, and the good thing about bad things is they also end.*
    —Anamaria Rabatte y Cervi                            _____

**15.** *Those who are of the opinion that money will do every-thing may very well be suspected to do everything for money.*
   —Sir George Savile                    _____

**16.** *Calamities are of two kinds: misfortune to ourselves, and good fortune to others.*
   —Ambrose Bierce                       _____

**17.** *When you can't be with the one you love, love the one you're with.*
   —Anonymous                            _____

**18.** *It is easy to get everything you want, provided you first learn to do without the things you cannot get.*
   —Elbert Hubbard                       _____

**19.** *Happiness can't buy money.*
   —Anonymous                            _____

**20.** *Comedy is simply a funny way of being serious.*
   —Peter Ustinov                        _____

**21.** *The forces that drive dramatic changes are often large, op-posing ideas that move slowly and ultimately press against one another with incredible force, like the techtonic plates responsible for continental drift and earthquakes.*
   —Al Gore                              _____

**22.** *It's not what you know that causes you trouble, it's what you know that ain't so.*
   —Anonymous                            _____

**23.** *The most amazing property and characteristic of life is its ability to move upstream against the flow of time. Life is the paradoxical contradiction to the second law (of thermody-namics), which states that everything is, always has been, and always will be running down to equilibrium and death.*
   —James Lovelock                       _____

**24.** *The unlived life is not worth examining.*
      —Anonymous                                    _____

**25.** *Laugh, and the world laughs with you;*
      *Weep and you weep alone.*
      —Ella Wheeler Wilcox                           _____

**26.** *It's always darkest just before the dawn.*
      —Anonymous                                    _____

**27.** *Every cloud has a silver lining.*
      —Anonymous                                    _____

**28.** *United we stand, divided we fall.*
      —Watchword of the American Revolution          _____

**29.** *If you're failing to plan, you're planning to fail.*
      —Anonymous                                    _____

**30.** *The higher you rise, the farther you fall.*
      —Anonymous                                    _____

**31.** *One of the greatest pieces of economic wisdom is to know what you do not know.*
      —John Kenneth Galbraith                        _____

**32.** *The biggest difference between L.A. and Edmonton was that instead of people looking at me I was looking at them.*
      —Wayne Gretzky                                 _____

**33.** *To not be upset over what you do not have, all you have to do is to ask what you do have.*
      —Ken S. Keyes, Jr.                             _____

**34.** *The most incomprehensible thing about the world is that it is comprehensible.*
      —Albert Einstein                               _____

**35.** *The improbable is extremely probable.*
     —Aristotle                                    _____

**36.** *Don't use no double negatives.*
     —Anonymous                                    _____

**37.** *Indecision is a form of decision.*
     —Conrad Black                                 _____


# HUMOR

Humor can be a serious business not only because it is an occupation that earns an increasing number of people a living but also because it is a necessary part of healthy living. People who earn their living by creating humor are adept at the game of opposites. Both paradox and humor are a flirtation with the absurd.

Humor helps distance us from the aggravations, troubles, and disasters of ordinary life. These days, high-stress companies are trying to get more of it into the workplace. Below are some jokes, witticisms, and wry observations that have paradox as a basis. Enjoy them and contribute to your sense of the paradoxical.

> An English lady, on being asked by a friend what she thought of her departed husband's whereabouts, replied, "Well, I suppose the poor soul is enjoying eternal bliss, but I wish you wouldn't talk about such unpleasant subjects."

> Harry was neither virtuous, young, nor handsome, and when he eventually died at a very advanced age he went to hell. A friend followed him soon after, but was astonished to find Harry sitting with a very beautiful young lady on his knee. "Harry," said the friend, "I thought this was hell I was entering, not heaven!" "It is," said Harry, "and I am her hell."

> As he reached the high school auditorium, the invited speaker of the day, a self-made man, got just the idea he

needed when he read the sign on the door, which said "Push." He pushed the door open, and he entered. As his speech to the students built to a crescendo, he exclaimed to them: "Turn around and look at the auditorium door. You'll read there in one word, on the sign on that door, the secret to how I got ahead." The students turned their heads and they looked at the door. The sign read "Pull."

The optimist goes to the window every morning and says, "Good morning, God." The pessimist goes to the window and says, "Good God! Morning."

"Beat me," begged the masochist. "No," answered the sadist.

"I wouldn't want to belong to any club that would accept me as a member."
—Groucho Marx

"He has all the virtues I dislike, and none of the vices I admire."
—Winston Churchill

"Blessed is he who expects nothing, for he will never be disappointed."
—Benjamin Franklin

"No good deed goes unpunished."
—Clare Boothe Luce

"Every society honors its live conformists—and its dead troublemakers."
—Mignon McLaughlin

"The fellow who thinks he knows it all is especially annoying to those of us who do."
—Harold Coffin

"Television has raised writing to a new low."
—Sam Goldwyn

"A pessimist is one who has been intimately acquainted with an optimist."
    —Elbert Hubbard

"Twixt the optimist and pessimist
The difference is droll:
The optimist sees the doughnut
But the pessimist sees the hole."
    —McLandburgh Wilson

"The optimist proclaims that we live in the best of all possible worlds; and the pessimist fears this is true."
    —James Branch Cabell

"A bank is a place where they lend you an umbrella in fair weather and ask it back when it rains."
    —Robert Frost

"This is not the end. It is not even the beginning of the end. But it is, perhaps, the end of the beginning."
    —Winston Churchill

"An atheist is a man with no invisible means of support."
    —John Buchan

"Smoking is one of the leading causes of statistics."
    —Kim Hubbard

"There are three types of people in this world. Those who can count, and those who can't."
    —Anonymous

A man goes to a doctor and says, "*Every*thing's wrong with me, but I don't know what it is. I touch my head and it hurts. I touch my chest and it hurts. I touch my leg and it hurts. What's the problem?" The doctor examines him and says, "Your finger's broken."

Feminist Anne Game says she laughed to learn that the owner of a topless car wash complains that too much press coverage is keeping embarrassed customers away from his business. Says Ms. Game, "It seems the less a woman is covered the more coverage she gets."—*Globe and Mail*, June 24, 1991

"Dame Edna" is one of England's greatest entertainment celebrities. She performs a several-hour solo act in London's most famous theaters, always to a jam-packed house. Her 1987 one-woman revue ran nine months and had the third-highest advance in the history of London's West End. A July 1991 *New Yorker* profile on Dame Edna said, "Dame Edna is a celebration of contradictions: hilarious and malign, polite and lewd, generous and envious, high and low comic. But the most sensational of the contradictions is that she is he." Dame Edna is a fifty-seven-year-old comic genius from Australia named Barry Humphreys. His Dame Edna character has become part of British folklore and culture.

The philosopher René Descartes had been having difficulty answering the questions from Jacques, the bartender of a local pub in Paris where, it seems, Descartes was in the habit of dropping in for a nightly drink. The bartender did not understand what Descartes meant when he had said, "I think, therefore I am." One evening he found out. Descartes entered the bar and Jacques asked, "The usual, Monsieur Descartes?" Descartes answered, "I think not" and instantly vanished.

The young Zen monk sees his master sitting motionless on a bench in the monastery garden, apparently deep in thought. "What are you thinking about?" asks the young monk. "I am thinking about the unthinkable," replies the master. "How can one think about anything that is unthinkable?" asks the young monk. "By not thinking," replies the master.

"Afraid of lung cancer? Relax, have a cigarette."
    —Cigarette ad

## LINGUISTIC PARADOXES

Phrases that use words in opposing meanings are purely linguistic but nevertheless amusing. Here are some examples of these good conditioners for the mind.

1. Your house can simultaneously burn up and burn down.
2. You fill in a form by filling it out.
3. Your alarm clock goes off by going on.
4. When the stars are out they are visible, but when the lights are out they are invisible.


## OXYMORONS, PALINDROMES, AND ANTINOMIES

Figures of speech such as oxymorons, palindromes, and antinomies are tools that help get your neural system used to working with opposites. They are good practice in looking at opposites, reversing them, and synthesizing them. Use them to practice the Paradox Process in the same way that business games help you practice business or team sports teach you about teamwork and competition.

An *oxymoron* is a phrase, usually of two words, that seems to make sense and not make sense at the same time because a contradiction exists or is sensed: for example, jumbo shrimp. A *palindrome* is a word, a sentence, or a number that reads the same backwards and forwards, or sometimes upside down. Nun and 69 are two examples. An *antinomy* is a contradiction between two equally valid principles, which are exact opposites: "Look before you leap" and "He who hesitates is lost." Such contradictions disturb people who find it difficult to accept the idea that two opposite principles can be equally valid, true, useful, or desirable.

The Paradox Process presupposes that you are able to recognize opposites and contradictions without difficulty. Since this skill can be developed even further by practice, read the following items, and with a friend or a group, see if you can add three more to each list.

## Oxymorons

| | |
|---|---|
| silent consent | people's democracy |
| cold sweat | small fortune |
| military intelligence | friendly divorce |
| civil servant | tough love |
| postal worker | merry widow |
| loud silence | jumbo shrimp |
| guest host | friendly fire |
| freezer burn | decaffeinated coffee |
| diet ice cream | white chocolate |
| holy war | living death |

## Palindromes

| | |
|---|---|
| Otto | peep |
| tot | radar |
| did | toot |
| mom | Madam |
| dad | Sex at noon taxes |
| gig | Rise to vote, sir! |
| bib | Able was I ere I saw Elba. |
| deed | Lager, Sir, is regal! |
| noon | |

I don't know whether words that read the same upside down are classed as palindromes, but while we're at it, why not? Here's one; can you add another?

pod

## Antinomies

A penny saved is a penny earned, but you have to spend money to make money.

Neither a borrower nor a lender be, but fly now and pay later.

# RIDDLES

What gets wetter as it dries? A few people are able to get the answer if they keep trying. Hint: The verb *dry* can be either transitive or intransitive.

(The answer, spelled backwards, is a *lewot.*)

# MOBIUS STRIP

Making and manipulating a Mobius strip (see Chapter 4) is a marvelous way to experience some of the strange aspects of paradox. It's a useful way of getting to a deeper level of consciousness. The Mobius strip is an eye-opener on the nature of opposites and paradox. It is easy to make a Mobius strip.

1. Cut two strips, each 1 inch wide and (approximately) 11 inches long, from a sheet of 8- by 11-inch paper.
2. Use adhesive tape to join two of the ends together to make a strip.
3. Twist one of the remaining ends by 180 degrees and tape the two ends together. This will give you a closed band about 11 inches long with a twist in it.

Having created this band with the twist in it, try to identify what is the inside and what is the outside. You'll find you can't. Each side is *both* the inside and the outside of the band. To prove this, draw a continuous line down the middle of the band, starting at any point. You'll find that your line runs down both the inside and the outside of the band. The effect is consternating, and it proves that two apparent opposites (in this case, inside and outside) can be one and the same thing—an assertion that mystics have been making for thousands of years.

If you want to surprise yourself even more, take a pair of scissors and cut the band in two along the line you have drawn. You'll find that instead of now having two bands, as you will have expected, you have only one 22-inch twisted band.

Now for the finale. Draw a line down the middle of this new band. Cut along this line. To your surprise there will now be two 22-inch bands and they are looped together.

## A FINAL AMBIGRAM

There is a card that has a sentence, the same sentence, printed on both sides. The sentence says, "The statement on the other side of this card is false." Is the statement true? To the paradoxical thinker, the answer is that it is both true and false, depending on how you look at it.

John Langdon has presented us with another example of something that is true and false at the same time, in the form of the ambigram shown below. Consciousness of the paradoxical character of everything is the first requirement for both wisdom and creativity. Try to think of more things that are both true and false.

1. _____

2. _____

3. _____

# Suggested Readings

Ackoff, Russel L. *Creating the Corporate Future*. New York: Wiley, 1981.

Adams, James L. *Conceptual Blockbusting*. San Francisco: W. H. Freeman, 1975.

Agor, Weston. *Intuitive Management*. Englewood Cliffs, N.J.: Prentice-Hall, 1984.

Barnard, Chester. *Functions of the Executive*. Cambridge: Harvard University Press, 1948.

Bergson, Henri. *Creative Evolution*. Westport, Conn.: Greenwood, 1975.

Burke, James. *Connections*. London: Macmillan, 1978.

Denbigh, K. G. *An Inventive Universe*. London: Hutchinson & Co., 1975.

Ford, Henry. *Today and Tomorrow*. Portland, Ore.: Productivity Press, 1988.

Gamache, R. Donald. *The Creativity Infusion*. New York: Random House, 1979.

Garfield, Patricia. *Creative Dreaming*. New York: Ballantine, 1976.

Gordon, William. *Synectics*. New York: Harper & Row, 1961.

Handy, Charles. *The Age of Paradox*. Cambridge: Harvard University Press, 1993.

Hudson, Liam. *Contrary Imaginations*. London: Methuen & Co., 1966.

Ihde, Don. *Experimental Phenomenology*. New York: Putnam, 1977.

Ijiri, Yuji, and Robert Lawrence Kuhn. *New Directions in Creative and Innovative Management*. Cambridge, Mass.: Ballinger, 1988.

Koestler, Arthur. *The Act of Creation*. New York: Macmillan, 1974.

Koestler, Arthur. *Janus*. New York: Random House, 1979.

Kuhn, Thomas. *The Structure of Scientific Revolutions*. Chicago: University of Chicago Press, 1962. Cambridge, Mass.: Ballinger, 1988.

Langdon, John. *Wordplay*. New York: Harcourt Brace Jovanovich, 1992. Out of print.

May, Rollo. *The Courage to Create*. New York: Norton, 1975.

Morgan, Gareth. *Imaginization: The Art of Creative Management*. Newbury Park, Calif.: Sage Publications, 1993.

Mueller, Gustav E. *The Interplay of Opposites*. New York: Bookman, 1956.

Naisbett, John. *Global Paradox*. New York: Avon, 1994.

Neill, Humphrey. *The Art of Contrary Thinking*. Caldwell, Ida.: Caxton, 1951.

O'Neil, John R. *The Paradox of Success*. New York: Putnam, 1994.

Ornstein, Robert E. *The Psychology of Consciousness*. New York: Viking, 1972.

Ornstein, Robert, and Paul Ehrlich. *New World, New Mind*. New York: Simon & Schuster, 1989.

Osborn, Alex. *Applied Imagination*. New York: Scribners, 1953.

Ring, Merrill. *Beginning with the Pre-Socratics*. Palo Alto, Calif.: Mayfield, 1987.

Rothenberg, Albert. *The Emerging Goddess: The Creative Process in Art, Science, and Other Fields*. New York: Norton, 1979.

Schneider, Kirk J. *The Paradoxical Self: Toward an Understanding of Our Contradictory Nature*. New York: Insight Books, 1990.

Schon, Donal A. *Invention and the Evolution of Ideas*. London: Tavistock Publications, 1963.

Schumaker, E. F. *Small Is Beautiful: A Study of Economics as If People Mattered*. London: Sphere Books Ltd., 1974.

Shmookler, Jacob. *Invention and Economic Growth*. Cambridge: Harvard University Press, 1966.

Swede, George. *Creativity*. Dayton: Wall and Emerson, 1993.

Vernon, P. E. (ed.). *Creativity: Selected Readings*. Middlesex, England: Penguin Books, 1970.

Wallas, Graham. *The Art of Thought*. New York: Harcourt, Brace, 1926.

Yukawa, Hideki. *Creativity and Intuition*. New York: Kodansha International, 1973.

# INDEX